GOD

GOD

❃

A Relationship Guide

By Judith E. Turian, Ph.D.

HAZELDEN®

Hazelden
Center City, Minnesota 55012
hazelden.org

Library of Congress Cataloging-in-Publication Data

Turian, Judith E., 1944–
    God : a relationship guide / Judith E. Turian.
        p.   cm.
    ISBN 978-1-59285-700-5 (softcover)
    1. Spirituality.   I. Title.
    BL624.T835 2009
    204'.4—dc22
                                        2008048582

Editor's note
The names, details, and circumstances may have been changed to protect the
privacy of those mentioned in this publication.
Alcoholics Anonymous and AA are registered trademarks of Alcoholics
Anonymous World Services, Inc.

The prayer on page 153 is excerpted from *Let Nothing Disturb You* by John
Kirvan. Copyright ©1996, 2007 by Quest Associates. Used with permission of
the publisher, Ave Maria Press, P.O. Box 428, Notre Dame, IN, 46556, www.
avemariapress.com.

The Prayer for Protection on page 148 was written by James Dillet Freeman.
Used by permission of Unity, www.unityonline.org.

12 11 10 09   1 2 3 4 5 6

Cover design by David Spohn
Typesetting by BookMobile Design and Publishing Services

In memory of Ruthie Farrell, aka "God's Wife,"
for her love, wisdom, and patience;
for teaching me everything I needed to know;
for being my surrogate mom;
for introducing me to God;
and for convincing me that He loves me
because I am His beloved child.

I will betroth you to myself forever,
betroth you with integrity and justice,
with tenderness and love.
I will betroth you to myself in faithfulness,
and you will come to know the Lord.
Hosea 2:19–20

Contents

Preface

I have wanted to write this book for many years. As a psychologist, I have come to believe that the best chance for recovery from any problem is found in a strong relationship with God. When you come to trust God as someone who can be called upon to help in times of trouble, guide in times of doubt, and provide meaning when nothing makes sense, you will find great hope in coping with any problems life presents.

Early in my career as a psychologist, I was on active duty in the U.S. Navy. It was not unusual for me to see a sailor for only two or three counseling sessions before his ship would go out to sea for months at a time. My patients obviously couldn't take me along on the cruise, so I wanted to offer them something that would be helpful when they were so far from home base.

Before long, I discovered, much to my surprise, that most of my patients had been brought up with faith and were open to talking about prayer and their relationships with God. It became clear to me that those who had faith could be taught ways to turn to God in times of stress and discouragement when they couldn't come for counseling. I found that I could give them some catchy expressions to use or simple exercises to follow that would help when they were overwhelmed, angry, afraid, or in turmoil. Over time, I picked up from others or developed for myself more and more of these memorable, simple, and helpful sayings and practices, many of which I'm sharing with you in this book.

During my service in the U.S. Navy, I became the clinical director of the Alcohol Rehabilitation Service at the Naval Hospital in Long Beach, California. In this capacity, I deepened my appreciation of the powerful medicine provided in the combination of spirituality, as outlined in the Twelve Step recovery programs, and psychotherapy.

I work with people from all walks of life and from a wide variety of ethnic, cultural, religious, and spiritual backgrounds. I have integrated the Twelve Step spirituality into my clinical practice, and it is rewarding to see the powerful healing that takes place as each person I help becomes more faithful to the spiritual path to which he or she has been led.

In my pursuit of spiritual growth, I began monthly meetings with a wise woman who used ancient methods for discerning the movement of the Holy Spirit in my life. Seeking to understand God's will in this way is found in many spiritual or religious paths and is known as spiritual direction. As my relationship with God deepened, I became interested in attending a formal ecumenical program leading to certification as a spiritual director. Using this training, I have worked with groups of people who are seeking greater depth in their relationships with God. I have also been able to add a new dimension to my clinical practice of psychology as I have been able to help patients to find or grow in faith.

Many people who come to me for help have wandered from their faith because they have become disappointed in God or feel betrayed by their church leadership or faith community. I assist in healing these divisions so that individuals can find their way back to God or to the spiritual fellowship of their choice. Often, people who come to me for help have no faith or only vague ideas about God. They are encouraged to find a God of their own understanding, "a Power greater than themselves" who can provide love, guidance, and support on life's often difficult journey.

Through recovery from my own life wounds, I have grown to be a strong and confident healer. I am able to be effective in helping others because I myself have lived through emotional pain and recovered. *God: A Relationship Guide* is the culmination of all that I have learned through life experience and professional training. This book is my way of passing on the lessons of my life.

Raised in a secular Jewish family, I was five at the time of my first spiritual experience, and I have been a seeker of God ever since. I learned about God in summer camp each year as I grew up, and I also attended Jewish Sunday School. I began watching Easter movies on television when I was eight or nine years old. I became fascinated with Jesus. By the time I reached my teens, I was asking God if Jesus really was His divine son, and if He was, to forgive me for not recognizing Him. After all, I was a young Jewish girl, and how could I have known? I loved visiting churches and cathedrals, especially when I traveled in Europe. I was inspired by medieval and Renaissance Christian art.

I led a life on the edge for many years, challenging God and living as if He didn't exist. When I finally came to my senses, I was inspired to turn my will and life over to God. It was then that I took the plunge and became Christian. It seems totally natural to me, as Jesus was a Jew and Christianity has its roots in Judaism. I think of myself as a completed Jew as I am no longer looking for the Messiah, but believe I have found Him.

I do believe, however, that God draws each of us to Him in a way that is right for us. I believe that He is more interested in our love and faithfulness than in the name of the path on which we walk.

I invite you to find, develop, and deepen your relationship with God through the experiences and lessons shared in this book. Because my personal spiritual path is that of Christianity, the ideas and language in this book are naturally colored by that perspective. As I believe that true spiritual wisdom is universal, this relationship guide invites the reader to apply the concepts expressed to any spiritual path that has at its center building a personal relationship with God.

It is important to note that I have used the traditional male pronoun for God to reflect my understanding of Him. However, I leave it to each of you to interpret God's gender—or lack thereof—according to your personal perception or understanding.

Acknowledgments

There are many people I know I should acknowledge, but I don't know who they are. I've been blessed with love and wisdom shared by many generous people whom I've met only briefly or have only heard speaking to groups of people and therefore never met at all. Often, they've given nuggets of insight gleaned from their life experiences or passed on memorable expressions that they may have heard from others on their paths. These have stuck with me so strongly that they've become a part of my soul and psyche, yet I have no recollection at all where I first heard them.

I fear that some sayings that I have used may be quotes or paraphrases of quotes written by authors or found in books unknown to me. I have tried to research possible sources, at times with no success. For this, I am truly sorry. In an attempt to make up for this, I have put together a list of suggested readings from which I believe many of my ideas may have originated. I don't claim to have even one original thought, though it is possible that I may have actually had a few here and there!

I would like to thank my life teachers whose names I do know. They include Father A., Mike Catanzaro, Mike Brubaker, Monsignor Terry Richey, Father Jim Hanley, Dottie Harris, and Sister Eileen Rafferty.

I also particularly want to thank my writing teacher, Mike Foley, and my writing group comrades including Joanne Andrew,

Ellen Estilai, Katrina Mason, and Nancy Van Dusen. They have been with me every step of the way, cheering me on and offering necessary but gentle criticism.

A special thanks goes to Sid Farrar for taking a chance on me and believing in the value of this book. He has been my editor, supporter, and all-around advisor throughout this process. Thanks also to Dave Spohn who designed the beautiful cover. The experience and professionalism of the Hazelden Publishing staff have turned the manuscript into the finished product you now hold in your hands.

When my home provided too many distractions from writing, I found the perfect atmosphere for accomplishing the task at my two favorite coffee houses in Redlands, CA. They are Fox Coffee House and Stell Coffee and Tea. I thank you both for allowing me to be a fixture on your premises while I wrote this book.

Finally, I could never have grown into the responsible, spiritual adult I am today and would never have had much of value to teach if it hadn't been for my second mom, Ruthie Farrell, and my loving, supportive friends Judith Barthel and Emma Mejico. I am grateful to you beyond measure.

. . .

Everything I have and all that I am is a gift from You, God. If there is any credit to be given, I give it to You. If only one person comes to know You, or returns to You or becomes more faithful or more intimate with You as a result of reading our book, it will be worth everything.

Thank You, God.

Chapter 1

Finding God in All the Wrong Places

I had thought God was dead. Didn't *Time* (4/8/66) magazine proclaim this from its ubiquitous cover?* God had been replaced by self-esteem, self-motivation, self-searching, self-examination, and especially by *ego*. God was my tall, handsome, blue-eyed therapist Jon whose hair transplants grew in rows like corn stalks and who was forever writing an important book about the existential self: *I AM I.* He was also the god of my friends. We all visited him once or twice a week, solo or as a flock, to discuss the sorry state of our individual or collective self-esteem and to complain or cry or rage against the life wounds, imagined or real, we had suffered that had brought us to our current pitiful state.

God was also my Iranian prince Ali, who would become my husband. He worked as a busboy at the corner Bagel Nosh, and he was going to become a famous writer as soon as he had enough money to keep him in paper and ink and enough drugs to stay continuously loaded. He had been preceded by a long line of boy-man gods, all of whom were going to make me happy, whole, and fixed. In fact, each of them served as my temporary fix.

It all began like this. From my earliest memory, I knew that I was born to be married at a young age to my prince, who would carry me off to our castle in the suburbs and make everything all right. In second grade, it was George Bell, who rode his bike to

*The cover of the April 8, 1966 issue said "Is God Dead?"

school every day. I didn't ride. Instead, I watched for him to go by, then dashed out the door with my lunch and my book bag and ran after him all the way to school.

Notice me. Notice me. Pleeease.

George never did notice me, but I fell in love with many others, always hoping to be loved, validated, and worthwhile. They each became my world, and I saw the universe and myself through their eyes. I existed only as someone's Girl. I felt loved and lovable as long as I had a man's arms around me.

But relationships required risk and vulnerability, letting someone else know me. I didn't even know myself. What would Steve or Joe or Chuck or Rick find out about me that I didn't yet know about myself? I always got out before that happened. I would leave before discovering for sure that I was not worthwhile, not lovable.

A friend once said to me, "Judith, to you, all men are gods."

I placed my self-esteem and my well-being in a man's hands. I looked to him for a fix to fill my emptiness. His job was to make me feel loved, intelligent, beautiful, interesting, hopeful, and whole. How could I ever feel these things without a man? And when a lover could no longer make me feel worthwhile, I had to move on. I could not find worthiness or esteem within.

I looked for God in all the wrong places, all the time, saying there was no God. But God became anything that could make me feel all right. If not a man, then someone's approval. If not approval, then success, more education, more degrees. If not these things, then a promotion. Or maybe it was being thinner, cuter, or having new clothes, new hair.

Eventually, it became evident that nothing outside of me could make me okay. I had become more and more dependent on people and things that gave me less and less satisfaction.

EGO = Edging God Out

While I was chasing after my many false gods, I was also busy trying to develop a strong sense of self. This was not, in itself, a bad thing. But for me, this meant that I had only myself to depend upon. I was it. There was no Heavenly Father, Creator, or Universal

Supreme Being to turn to. There was no effective divine partnership to reliably help me through the rough times, to bless the peaceful or joyous days, to give me reason to know that I was, in fact, worthwhile and lovable. This was a lonely place to be.

Searching for and finding God in all the wrong places was my way of filling my "God hole." I believe we all have a deep spiritual yearning for God to give our lives meaning. Whatever I was making into a god—whether it was me, a man, a goal, an achievement, a substance, someone's approval, or God Himself—would become the fundamental organizing principle of my life. I had to choose which it would be. I chose God. Thank God for that!

"Thou Shalt Have No Other Gods before Me"

Sometimes I think my mind is out to mug me. Just let me focus on something I think I must have to be happy or on someone I believe I'll be miserably unhappy if I lose, and an obsession will be lurking in the shadows gaining tornado strength.

I must have a new car. Sure, mine is operating just fine. But it's got a lot of miles on it, and I travel a long distance to my office over a difficult road. I mean I have to be safe, right? And it's imperative to get to work. After all, no work, no money. So the vehicle should be reliable. And I've had other cars that have died at about this mileage.

So I start shopping. It has to be a good deal on the right car with all the necessary equipment and the perfect interior and exterior. I read through the papers. I go online and look at *Kelley Blue Book, Consumer Reports,* and *Consumer Guide.* I check out AutoTrader.com and craigslist. I read and research. I am anxious and excited. I don't sleep enough. I can hardly focus on the simplest activities of daily living.

. . .

Or, I had a date with a guy. He says he had a great time, and he's going to call. I wait by the phone, check my e-mail. I can't stop thinking about him. He's so nice, so intelligent, so polite. Yes, it's true that he says he doesn't want a serious relationship right now.

He has to say that, doesn't he? That could change, couldn't it?

I am drowning in adrenaline. My stomach is doing flip-flops. I feel like throwing up. My heart is pounding, and I can barely catch my breath. I am so afraid.

Now where will I find someone to love me?

. . .

Alternately, I'm hurt and angry. I've been doing a great job at work, producing more than anyone. I'm dedicated, go the extra mile. People like me. So why is my boss always hanging out with the new guy at the clinic? How come he gets all the attention and recognition? I can't stop thinking about what a jerk my boss is.

He'll realize how valuable I am, and then he'll be sorry he didn't give me the attention and approval I deserve. Won't he?

. . .

The car, the guy, and the boss's approval are all false gods. And what all these scenarios have in common is that the obsession (nonstop freight train thinking) is dictating what I think, how I feel, and ultimately, how I'll act. My world has become organized around the obsession, and my well-being depends on the outcome being the way I need it to be. The obsession has now become my god, and I have broken the commandment that says "Thou shalt have no other gods before me."

"Spiritual Drano," or Practice Makes Perfect

I have learned that whatever I rehearse in my mind becomes my reality. If I'm practicing a problem, all I get is a perfect problem with all the associated disruptive emotions. But if I focus away from whatever is troubling me and think about God or something spiritual instead, my mind gets cleared so that God can inspire me with a solution or at least free me from the negative feelings.

Lots of times, when I have a problem brewing that I don't want to focus on, I create a new problem by becoming obsessed with something totally unrelated. Often, I do this unconsciously. My friend is sick or my child's grades have gone down the tubes, so my mind becomes overly attached to something I can manage, such as buying a car.

On other occasions, I'll try to figure out why something is or isn't happening. That guy I like hasn't called me back or the boss is ignoring me. When I can't come up with an answer, do I drop it? Of course not!

I think longer and harder about it. And, instead of calming down, as I might have if a satisfactory solution or explanation had become apparent or if I had accepted that I couldn't change the situation, I focus even more on it. Before you know it, I have a good obsession going. I have practiced the problem in my mind until it has truly become a perfect problem.

I've become an emotional wreck. My thinking channels are clogged with sticky, dark gunk made by fear, anxiety, or anger. I need something like Roto-Rooter to flush them out so that God can bring a fresh flow of divine ideas, which might even carry a solution. Time to reach for "Spiritual Drano." Instead of rehearsing the problem, I must focus on the solution, which is God. Repeating thoughts of God will clear the goop of obsession and negativity from the passages in my mind. Repeated treatments might be needed before peace and calm can be restored.

How to Use Spiritual Drano

Using Spiritual Drano is a lot like pulling weeds. Have you ever gone away for a while and come back to find a yard full of weeds? You get up the next morning determined to get rid of the weeds before they totally take over and nothing healthy can grow. So you spend hours pulling weed after weed until it feels like your back is about to break. When you look out at the yard the next morning, it looks as if you never even pulled the first weed. So you go at it for another full day and seem to make a little headway. You have to keep up the effort steadily until, after many treatments, you only have to do a little maintenance weed pulling.

Negative thoughts and obsessions are like weeds of the mind. If you aren't diligent about pulling these thought weeds, they will block out the fresh air, water, and sunshine needed for healthy solutions to develop.

Spiritual Drano is the recommended treatment for drainage of stinking thinking sewage. Every time a problem comes to mind and I can't seem to stop thinking about it, I repeat a short spiritual phrase ten times over, focusing on it with all my heart, soul, and mind. Then I force my attention on something else. When the obsessive thoughts return in two or three seconds, which they usually do, I start all over again. Sometimes I have to do this a thousand times a day. This is an easy direction, but it's hard to follow because it requires dogged perseverance. The payoff is that, after a while, I'm able to think about the things I want to think about, and I no longer have to think about the things I don't want to think about. That's real freedom.

Here are some phrases I use to break an obsession:

> *God is in charge.*
> *I'm a good person, and God loves me.*
> *God is my all. I know no fear.*
> *God, help me.*
> *God is my health. I can't be sick.*
> *There is no power in this world greater than my God.*

You can come up with some of your own phrases to use, affirmations that meaningfully reflect your own spiritual path. Once you're no longer thinking of the problem, God will have an opening to bring forth a solution.

But first, you need to get to know God so that you can recognize the solution when it's given and connect it with divine purpose.

Chapter 2

Getting to Know God

So where do you start when you're empty and willing? Right there where you find yourself. "God or Sam or Jesus or Fred or Allah or Jane or whatever Your name is, if You're really there, show me in a way I can understand." I wanted to believe, but I was so scared.

What if He disapproved of me? What if He was fed up with me? What if He punished me? What if He ignored me, wasn't interested in me? What if He didn't understand me? What if He wouldn't love me or think I was worthwhile or take care of me? What if He was like my mom, who was powerful but critical, judgmental, distant, and nonvalidating? What if He was a big joke or He didn't really exist?

Whoops. Now fear was my god!

The truth of the matter is that I'd always believed in the existence of God. I'd even had some religious education. Sometimes I prayed, but I had no better idea how to have a close relationship with Almighty God than I did with any of the almighty men I'd worshipped.

I started by listening to what others had to say about God, and I very slowly began to work my way toward Truth and Understanding and Relationship and Faith and Belief and Trust.

The first thing I heard that made sense to me was to pretend that God was a warm, loving, and tender daddy who not only wanted what was good for me but also knew what was good for me and had the power to deliver it. This was not a major stretch for me, since my own dad was warm, loving, and tender. I always felt safe with him, though he was not a powerful kind of guy.

The next important thing I learned was that a relationship with God couldn't grow if I didn't give it time and attention. It would be like meeting someone who seemed interesting and whom I thought I would like to know better. We could exchange phone numbers or e-mail addresses, but if I were too lazy to call or too busy to meet for lunch or to hang out, no relationship would ever develop, regardless of how much the other person might desire to know me.

Once I decided to give God some of my time (big of me, huh?), I had to get willing to let Him know me, to be vulnerable with Him. But wait, this didn't make sense. *If He's God and He supposedly knows everything about me, why did I have to tell Him anything?*

A close friend of mine put it this way.

"Judith," she said. "When someone calls you because she is having problems, and she trusts you to listen and give honest, sound guidance, don't you feel complimented?"

"Well, sure," I said.

Then my friend informed me that God feels the same way. Though He already knows what's happening in my life and what I'm thinking and feeling, He likes it when I take the time to tell Him about it myself. That's the start of opening a channel of communication for me to receive guidance from God about the things I have taken to Him.

God Doesn't Make Junk

I began talking to God, telling Him about how my day had gone and what was planned for the next day. I thanked Him for keeping me from making a jerk out of myself with my boss and for helping me be kind to my co-worker, whom I would've preferred to get shipped off to Siberia for good. I asked Him to show me how to be appropriate at the upcoming staff meeting and to give me control over my desire to flirt with the gorgeous navy chaplain who was single but very much a priest.

Most of all, I begged His forgiveness for falling so short of how I thought He would want me to be. I didn't feel worthy to kneel before Him. Instead, I would fling myself on the floor and sob for being such "a dirty rat." And then I'd feel His gentle touch and His peace.

In time, I came to realize that God creates anyone He wants to create. He chose to create me, and as far as I know, God doesn't make junk.

A Thimbleful of Spiritual Knowledge

I was a newly commissioned officer in the U.S. Navy when I came to California. I arrived with three suitcases, two cats, one litter box, an assortment of student furniture, and more debt than I could hope to cover on my beginning officer's salary.

I called Consumer Credit Counselors of Los Angeles and went to see one of their debt counselors. I was told that the agency could not help me unless I had additional income. Further, I was told that I had about six months until my creditors caught up with me and that I should have a part-time job lined up by then, in addition to my work in the navy.

I was in a panic, and I turned for advice from Ruthie, a new acquaintance who would later become my dear friend and mentor. She was a five-foot-two dynamo with silver hair, elegant dress, proper manners, acerbic wit, and so much wisdom that I thought she might be God's wife.

Ruthie became a surrogate mother to me, helping me to finally become an adult. She demonstrated the value of a relationship with God by the way she lived, and she was one of the first people to introduce me to God. For twenty-two years, until the day she died, Ruthie remained my confidant and advisor, closer to me than my own skin.

She was actually the wife of a Marine Corps colonel pilot who had flown in three wars. She took me under her wing as a fresh lieutenant JG (junior grade) naval officer, and she taught me how to navigate my new and mysterious navy world appropriately. A side benefit, I thought, was that if she was married to her marine for thirty-plus years, maybe she could help me figure out how to snag and keep one for myself!

When I described my financial situation to Ruthie, she informed me that if my creditors did, in fact, catch up with me and if I was not taking care of my debt, my navy command would find out. If that happened, she said, it would not go well for me. Thus began my first amazing lesson in knowing God.

Ruthie suggested that I sit quietly and review in my mind everything that I knew about God (which, believe me, at that time wasn't much). Then I was to read something spiritual, tell God my need, and thank Him in advance for answering my prayer.

So I thought about what little I knew about God. He is good. I am His child, He loves me, and He wants me to be happy. It is His good pleasure to share His creation with me *because* I am His child. If I pray believing, He will answer my prayer. That was the sum of all that I knew, and it was enough.

Next, I chose a scripture passage to read. It assured me that God knows what I need and that if I placed God and His way of holiness first in my life, He would take care of all my needs. The reading also told me that I didn't have to worry.

Finally, I told God that I had a lot of debt that I wanted to be able to repay without making more debt. I had to find a part-time job within six months in order to begin accomplishing this goal. Then I thanked God for answering my prayer.

I read that passage and thanked God for prayers answered every day for six months. By that time, my creditors had indeed found me, I had a part-time job, and I had a contract with Consumer Credit Counselors. And I continued to read and thank God every day for the next four years until the debt was paid.

Remember that you do not need to know a lot about God or have a lot of prayer experience for this method to work. If you have only a thimbleful of spiritual knowledge and use it all, you will be more successful at demonstrating answers to prayer than the person who has a barrelful of spiritual knowledge and only uses a thimbleful.

How to Use Your Thimbleful (or More)
of Spiritual Knowledge

Try this method for yourself in any area where you need higher-octane power than you can come up with on your own. Whatever endeavor you have that seems overwhelming, whatever need you have that you've just not been able to fill, whatever goal you've been trying to accomplish yet somehow can't quite reach, try this technique. You could ask for help in overcoming a character trait such as procrastination or perfectionism. Perhaps you've been trying unsuccessfully to lose weight, quit smoking, or be on time. Maybe you find it hard to live within your means and you keep spending money you don't have at your disposal or buying things you don't really need. Or maybe being able to save for a down payment on a mortgage keeps eluding you.

Here are the steps to take:

1. Review in your mind what you know about your God.
2. Pick a spiritual reading from your path and read it. Selections could come from the Bible, the Koran, metaphysical writings, Twelve Step literature, or the mystics or saints or theologians from any path.
3. Confide in God about your need or problem or goal. Ask Him for help, believing that He can and will provide it.
4. Then, thank God in advance for prayers answered.
5. Keep reading and continue to thank God every day until His help is fully demonstrated in your life.

As you experience success and positive outcomes using your thimbleful (or more) of spiritual knowledge, you will find yourself beginning to trust God.

Chapter 3

Getting to Trust God

*O*nce I was talking to God, the next question was what to say. Just how much did I want Him to know? How open was I to listening to Him? What was I going to trust Him with? Was God going to be trustworthy or would He let me down?

I had to learn that trust comes with experience. When I meet someone new, do I pour out my whole heart? Do I expect my new friend to be loyal or trustworthy? Maybe I do, perhaps not. Either way, it takes time and trials to know how much I can trust this person who is becoming my friend.

Slowly, with repeated experience and many tests over time, I find my new friend and I have become well known to one another, trusted companions. Over time, we not only share interests but also come to confide in one another our joy, pain, successes, and struggles with relationships, parents, children, bosses, co-workers, school, self-esteem, money, and faith.

It works exactly the same way with God. The more I let Him into my life and the more chances I gave Him to be a good friend to me, the more I came to trust Him.

The truth is that we often make the same mistakes with God as in all our other relationships. After all, we bring to God the same limitations or assets we display in our relationships with people.

If you're someone who rushes headlong into a relationship, as I often did, trusting before gaining evidence of the other's trustworthiness, hoping to be taken care of without taking responsibility for yourself, and then getting angry when the other lets you down, then there's a good chance you'll do the same with God. If you're a person who finds it difficult to trust others, you'll have difficulty trusting God. Or perhaps your style is to hold back, waiting for enough data that proves that the other is trustworthy, but regardless of how much evidence you get, it's never enough. That's what will happen when you try to build a relationship with God.

If you're defensive in your relationships with people, you'll be defensive with God. If you're argumentative, have a need to always be right or have the last word; if you're shy and reserved; if you're cold, distant, arrogant, or abrasive; if you have perfectionistic demands of others or feel like others can't do anything without your help; if you're open, loving, communicative, and nondefensive—any trait that you normally display in relationships with others will probably also play a role in your relationship with God.

We tend to expect God to have the same feelings or beliefs about us that we experienced from our parents or other powerful individuals in our early lives. If your father was critical, aggressive, or abusive, you will likely expect God to be that way. If your mother coddled you and never found any fault with you or set any limits for you, that's what you'll expect from God.

If your parents were distant and unexpressive, well, you'll probably think that God is that way. Perhaps consequences were delivered in your home quickly and consistently with no chance for talk or explanation. In that case, and particularly if you grew up in a Catholic family, you might expect God to be a big accountant in the sky busily counting "venials, mortals, and indulgences," or awarding merit badges for good deeds and demerits for mild and serious sins, delivering swift reward and punishment with little concern for your feelings.

If your parents were busy working or taking care of several children and seemed to have no time for you, you'll believe that God has more important things to worry about than you and your problems. If you were fortunate and experienced affection, trust, respect, and openness in your family, then it will be easier for you to believe that God is a loving being who cares about you, one whom you can trust.

As a result of our earlier relationship experiences, we push God away or expect Him to harm us, reject us, ignore us, or disapprove of us. Conversely, we might get angry when our unreasonable expectations for special treatment aren't met. We assume that God will give us everything we want, never allowing us to have painful experiences or feelings. Once we learn how to have healthier relationships, whether through good example, the good fortune of inheriting an even temperament, life experience, or the hard work of self-examination in counseling or prayer, we will come to trust God and know that He will take care of us and be there for us no matter what.

Repeats-for-Correction

I've come to believe that God loves us and wants us to be happy and successful in life. He allows us to repeat our mistakes in any area of our lives until we learn the lessons that must be learned. Once we stop trying to make an unsuccessful behavior, relationship, or attitude work and decide to change, we no longer have to repeat the painful process. We become free to be the best we can be and all that God wants us to be.

When I find myself in the midst of an old pattern that has been painful for me in the past, I try to recognize it as an opportunity for a repeat-for-correction. Changes in the area of personal character, behavior, family, emotions, or work may be painful but necessary and, in the end, well worth the trouble.

One of my first repeats-for-correction had to do with how I conducted myself in a relationship with a man. Shortly after I decided to make God my friend, I began dating a young marine enlisted "grunt" who probably loved the idea of having captured the attention of an older, though certainly not wiser, officer doc. This relationship followed the same recipe my previous ones did— swift, intense, and ultimately disappointing. I thought I was in love without bothering to get to know him. I was planning our wedding and our lives together when it would have been better to plan what to do that evening, what to wear, what I wanted to find out about him, or what I wanted to tell him about me. Of emotional, intellectual, and spiritual intimacy there was little.

The good thing was that since I'd begun to trust God, I had become teachable. After only two short months, I learned an important lesson. I realized that I was always putting the cart before the horse, the end result being the illusion of love, not the real thing. When a man put his arms around me, I interpreted the accompanying good feelings as love.

Friendship has to come first. I had to learn to approach men as friends instead of potential husbands and saviors. I didn't understand that it takes a long time to get to know another person. I had to separate the real person from my fantasy. I so much wanted to believe that this man was *the one* that I often saw what I wanted to see, not the reality. I denied what I knew to be true about a person in favor of a belief in his "potential" or an unreasonable faith that he would change for love.

I have gone through many repeats-for-correction, not only in my relationships with men, but in all areas of my life where improvement has been needed. After getting completely out of debt, I found myself overspending again. I found it harder to maintain the discipline I had learned once I was earning more money. I had to get back to basics, and because of my earlier success, I knew what to do.

When I was in the navy and later when I was working for a corporation, I found myself losing sight of my primary purpose of helping others in favor of trying to gain more power and recognition within the organization. This caused me particular stress as I began adopting behaviors and attitudes that reflected the culture of the company. In the process, I stopped behaving and thinking in a manner that was authentic for me.

I had begun doing the power-seeking thing yet again when Ruthie, by now my dear friend and mentor, brought me up short. She reminded me of the saying, "Shoemaker, stick to thy last."

In other words, focus on my profession, what I had been trained to do. Be of service. Help others. Once I had made that decision, a perfect opportunity came along. Previously, I might have passed up that chance, scoffing at the fact that there was no corporate ladder to climb. However, since I had learned the necessary lessons, I was able to make a change that allowed me to avoid the power trap and be true to myself.

With each repeat-for-correction, I've had the opportunity to grow and change. As each lesson has been learned, that problem hasn't had to occur again. God has always been right there to teach me what I needed to learn at a pace that enabled me to absorb it.

God Does for Us What We Can't Do
for Ourselves

I decided to make a commitment to God to approach men only in friendship for ninety days. My first attempt at this new plan was with Bob, a tall, handsome navy surgeon with a great smile and a shy manner. We worked together, talked together, and laughed together. We were both new in faith and shared our budding relationships with God.

But could I leave this alone?

No-o-o-o!

I became convinced that God meant us to be together, that he was *the one*. I told God that I knew I had made this vow to Him, but since it must be His will that my navy captain doctor and I be together, He would surely make allowances if I cheated a bit on the promise.

So my future husband (totally in my own mind and unbeknownst to him, of course) and I took off to the Colorado River with a bunch of other navy folks from the hospital where we worked. We were going camping.

When we arrived at our campsite, my cross fell off my necklace into the dirt. This cross had been a Christmas gift from my marine "grunt," and it was really the first outward symbol of my new faith. It was important to me, and I began desperately searching for it. The night was pitch black, so I borrowed a flashlight and began frantically going over and over this expanse of dirt with my heart pounding and a sinking feeling in my stomach. After a long, dark hunt, I found it. I fervently thanked God and began wondering if He was trying to get my attention. (Sometimes that's the way God talks to me—through my thoughts, my intuition, my gut, or even coincidence.) I immediately discounted that idea as silly.

The next day, I suggested to Bob, who was about to become my knight in shining armor (if he didn't watch out), that we find a spot of our own, away from the river and the crowd. He agreed at first, and I was thrilled. But later that evening, he said that he'd prefer to wake up early by the river and watch the sunrise. My plan was foiled, and God prevailed.

I learned that when I haven't got the human strength to follow my heart and please God, He steps in and gives me the power I need. He has often done for me what I could not do for myself.

I felt sorrow that I'd been so easily diverted by my self-will but awed by how incredibly trustworthy God proved to be.

How to Identify and Cope
with Repeats-for-Correction

When my patients complain about a feeling they are experiencing in reaction to something going on in their lives, I usually ask them if they have ever reacted to a situation or a person with similar emotions. I also ask what thoughts are going through their minds. Has anyone in the past ever spoken to them in this manner? If so, this might be an opportunity to identify a repeat-for-correction.

I have noticed in my own life, and in the lives of others as well, that I am often deep into a repeat-for-correction before I recognize what's going on. Sometimes I have been so completely oblivious to this opportunity for life change that it has passed me by before even a dim awareness of it comes to my mind.

When I was working for the Alcohol Rehabilitation Service at the Naval Hospital, a nurse who was very opinionated and senior in rank to me (a bad combination, in my mind) was transferred to our unit. It seemed to me that every time I made a suggestion or outlined a procedure that I thought should be followed, she disagreed with me. If I actually went to her to get her input or advice, she took over and began to give me directions or orders. I am an outspoken person, but I felt run over or diminished whenever I was around her. I wanted her respect, approval, *and* to get my way. I got none of those things. I couldn't even begin to let go before I realized that my reactions to this nurse were very similar to the way I used to react to my older sister.

How often we recreate in the workplace our position in our family of origin. The boss becomes our authoritarian father. A senior co-worker becomes a nurturing mother. We might be rebellious toward or afraid of the disapproval of one and needy of the other's protection. Other co-workers become our siblings, and we suddenly find ourselves being labeled as Miss Goody Two-Shoes, or acting out for attention, or desperately trying to avoid notice, or making everyone laugh, or becoming the butt of everyone's jokes or the receiver of blame. Once we can identify how we're reacting and why, we can begin to change.

At times, it's the thoughts more than the feelings or behaviors that show us that a repeat is in progress. We have tapes running in our heads repeating the messages we heard from our parents or other influential people in our lives:

- I am "so beautiful" and "so smart" that I don't have to put in any effort at work or at school to succeed.
- I am "such an idiot." How could I have ever thought that I could get that promotion?
- I'll "never amount to anything."
- No matter how hard I try to get her approval, I won't because I'm "worthless."
- Why do I bother? I'm bound to be a "failure."
- I am so "special." If you knew who I am, you would never treat me this way!

It is important to recognize this negative or arrogant self-talk and change it. It is also necessary to identify who taught it to us.

Mom, Dad, siblings, teachers, coaches, friends, lovers, spouses, bosses, church leaders, culture—anyone who had power in our lives could have given us untrue messages about ourselves which we swallowed hook, line, and sinker. Most of us have come to believe these ideas about ourselves so deeply that they might as well have been encoded in our genetic material.

My dad thought I could do no wrong, so I expected others to be unreasonably impressed with me. On the other hand, I could never get my mother's approval. So I attracted people in my life who wouldn't give me approval.

I, like most other people I've met, brought into my life unfinished business from the past, and I subsequently fell in love with it, married it, or went to work for it or with it. It's as if we have radar inside that unfailingly singles out individuals who can bring about a repeat-for-correction.

I can sabotage a potentially good relationship with my false beliefs about myself or with my defensive fear and anger. I can stay in a harmful relationship because I firmly hold the belief that I can make the other person change and give me what I need. Or I might discern the truth about a relationship as helpful or harmful, loving or demeaning, but I discount my own perceptions or feelings as untrue, invalid, silly, or exaggerated.

What is to be done about recognizing and coping with repeats-for-correction so we don't have to keep doing the same painful things over and over and over? Use the chart on the next page to help you do this. Instructions for using it are on page 22.

Asking God to Reveal the Truth about Myself
and the Person or Situation Bothering Me

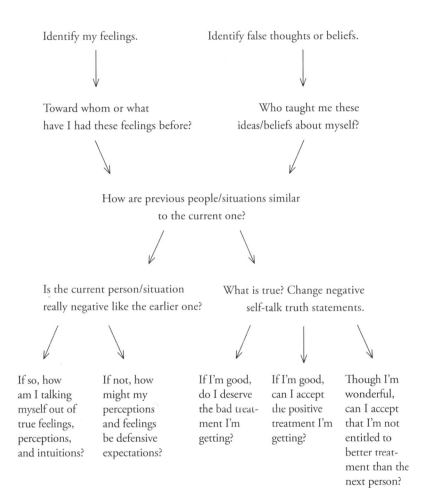

Identify my feelings.

Toward whom or what
have I had these feelings before?

Identify false thoughts or beliefs.

Who taught me these
ideas/beliefs about myself?

How are previous people/situations similar
to the current one?

Is the current person/situation
really negative like the earlier one?

What is true? Change negative
self-talk truth statements.

If so, how
am I talking
myself out of
true feelings,
perceptions,
and intuitions?

If not, how
might my
perceptions
and feelings
be defensive
expectations?

If I'm good,
do I deserve
the bad treat-
ment I'm
getting?

If I'm good,
can I accept
the positive
treatment I'm
getting?

Though I'm
wonderful,
can I accept
that I'm not
entitled to
better treat-
ment than the
next person?

At every step of the way, talk to God and to another trusted person who understands what you are trying to do. Is this a repeat-for-correction? What lesson is here for me to learn?

Instructions for Using the Chart

Identify Your Feelings.
- Have you had these feelings before?
- Who or what were you reacting to when you had these feelings in the past?
- How is the person or situation you're reacting to now similar to the person or situation from the past?
- Is this person or situation you have currently drawn into your life really harmful or toxic for you?
- If so, your repeat-for-correction will involve discovering how you discount yourself by talking yourself out of your feelings, perceptions, or gut intuition.
- If not, your feelings may actually be serving as a defense against repeating past experiences that are incorrectly influencing your current perceptions.

Identify False Thoughts or Beliefs about Yourself.
- Who taught you to think about yourself in exaggerated negative or positive terms, causing you to have unrealistic expectations of negative or positive outcomes in your life?
- How is the current situation or person similar to circumstances or people who first taught you these beliefs?
- What is really true about you? Change your untrue self-talk to truth statements (even if you don't fully believe them).
    - "It is true that I'm smart (beautiful, creative), but that doesn't exempt me from having to work for a positive outcome."
    - "I'm a good, worthwhile, and loving person. I can have success (approval, love) in my life."
- The repeat-for-correction occurs in making one of these decisions.
    - "If I'm good, do I deserve the bad treatment I'm getting?"
    - "If I'm good, can I accept the positive treatment I'm getting?"
    - "If I'm as wonderful as I think I am, can I accept that I'm not entitled to better treatment than the next person?"

As you practice the skills to help you identify and understand your repeats-for-correction, you'll find that you are more able to make good choices and avoid old pitfalls. Relationships will be more rewarding, and your reactions to people and circumstances in your life will be more balanced. As you gain greater confidence in yourself and trust in God to continue to be on your side, you'll be able to risk entering into a deeply loving relationship. And there is God, waiting patiently and expectantly for your love.

Chapter 4

Getting to Love God,
or My New Boyfriend, God

I was excited about my new relationship with God. I poured out my heart to Him and begged His forgiveness for turning my back on Him. I alternated between tears of sorrow and tears of joy and love. Long after God had forgiven me—for I believe pardon comes as soon as we ask for it—I was carrying on about my defects and past failures. It was as if God's forgiveness came too easily, and I needed to punish myself more.

At first, it seemed I couldn't make a mistake. Whatever I wanted, I got. If I prayed for something, it was delivered before I could blink an eye. If I even thought about straying from the moral high road, God intervened before any damaging action or painful results had a chance to occur.

I received help from God in every imaginable way. I had enough money to pay my bills. Friends gave me quality hand-me-down clothing so I only had to buy my navy uniforms. My patients liked me and seemed to improve, despite the fact that I often felt that I had no idea what I was doing. I kept my mouth shut with my boss, co-workers, friends, or guys when saying what was really on my mind would surely get me into a world of trouble. All that I might have asked for seemed to be granted before the words had taken form in my mind. Like the devoted suitor

He was, God knew just how to go about drawing me closer to Him in the early years of our love affair.

Yes, I did say love affair, for my thoughts and feelings about God were not very different from those I experienced in the days when I had made men my god. I was obsessed with God. I wanted Him all to myself and to be with Him all the time. I tried to change myself in whatever way necessary to gain His love and His approval.

I bragged to my friends about our relationship, and I wanted everyone else to love God and be excited for me. I was obnoxious, overbearing, and boring, just as I'd often been when in the initial stages of a relationship with a man.

I felt loved, accepted, validated, and appreciated. Whatever was wrong with me had been fixed, I was quite sure. The whole world went away, and there was just God and me. I prayed, I read, I went to church and on retreats. These were my dates with God. I was being courted, it seemed, and I was totally lost in love.

I don't know about you, but when I'm in love, I want to please my lover. This is particularly true if he happens to be all-powerful, all-loving, everywhere present, and to have a wonderful plan for me.

Unzip Your Godsuit, or You Are Lovable Because God Loves You

I was on fire with love, and I couldn't understand why everyone didn't feel the way I did. Moreover, I acted as if my closeness to God entitled me to push the truth according to Judith on everyone I encountered. I was in the running for sainthood and mother superior of my immediate world.

Saint Judith. It has quite a ring to it, don't you think?

First of all, I became a candidate for Scrupulous Anonymous. Is there such a thing? There ought to be for people like I was when I was trying to be so perfect. I had to read certain meditation books every morning. Then I was required to read scripture. Then it was mandatory to quietly meditate on what I had read for thirty to forty-five minutes and write about it. If I didn't do this ritual, I was afraid my day would not go right. Then I had to review my day at night to see where I had erred.

Don't get me wrong. These are wonderful practices followed by the most spiritual and godly people throughout the ages. The problem was that I wasn't allowed (By whom? Surely only myself!) to deviate.

I had to go to church every Sunday and take communion. I had to go to confession, though there was little of interest to confess. After all, I was loving, kind, honest, chaste, giving, and prayerful. I helped others. I was a hard worker. In fact, I worked harder, in my unbiased opinion, than anyone else around. And I told this to my boss, as if this were the most appropriate thing in the world to say. I wore my navy uniform perfectly and proudly. I always had a good attitude, smiled, and supported my navy command in every way that I was asked.

I "helped" my friends by telling them that their relationship with God should be stronger, that they should allow God to discipline their drinking, eating, spending, sex life. Heaven knows, if they continued their misguided behaviors and attitudes, they were headed for disaster.

How could they keep that extra three cents change they had been mistakenly given at the supermarket checkout? How could they read only one meditation book and say a quick prayer before leaving home for work in the morning and consider this sufficient? How could they criticize their commanding officer or the church hierarchy?

If I were the only example of a so-called godly or spiritual person whom others encountered, it would be no wonder if they didn't want to know God better. For all my talk of God's love, I acted as if He were nothing if not judgmental, harsh, and punitive. The God that I presented to others was just another self-centered parent whose approval could never be won, even if perfection was achieved.

I was just so in love with God and so busy, in my own misguided way, trying to please Him that I couldn't see myself. I was filled with spiritual pride, being a know-it-all, thinking I was better than everyone else when it came to a relationship with God. I thought I was on a higher spiritual plane than most of the mortals with whom I came in contact.

I told a priest that he drank too much. I told friends how to pray if they *really* wanted results. I told the addictions counselors who worked for me how to conduct themselves in their personal relationships: *You can't date that girl. She has too little sobriety. You have to get the emotional, intellectual, and spiritual together with him before you become sexual.* It's not that what I had to say was necessarily wrong. It's just that it was none of my business. I was dispensing advice without being asked.

Not surprisingly, people began running in the opposite direction when they caught sight of me. It seemed that people weren't interested in "the way, the truth, and the light" according to Saint Judith.

The true Good News, I learned over time, is that God loves me exactly as I am. God's love isn't something I deserve or earn. I have it just *because* I am. God might not like my choices or behavior or attitudes or lack of love, but there's nothing in the world I can do or say that will change my worth in His eyes. I am lovable *because* God made me and loves me.

I believe that the same is true for everyone.

It's difficult to say when or exactly how I learned this and came to deeply believe it. Like most things worthwhile in my life, I probably heard it from someone else, read it, or was subtly taught it by that "still small voice" within that I call the Holy Spirit. I became open to learning through experience, both my own and that of others. I know that God often expresses His love for me through others who don't stop loving me when I do something wrong, when I'm less than perfect, when I contradict myself by saying one thing and doing another. Instead they hold me, help me, encourage me, and love me no matter what.

When I finally learned these lessons, I was able to stop judging myself so harshly. The more I accepted myself as the flawed but lovable person that I am, the more I could accept others as lovable in God's eyes, and I no longer had a need to judge them. They could get through life just fine without my opinions and directions.

I had unzipped my godsuit, and I was free.

Love Brings Up Everything Opposite to Itself
So That Love Can Heal It

During the days when I was looking for God in all the wrong places, I went to a psychologist for help. I was in therapy for a long time, but I never got out of "the blame game." If only my mother had been more gentle and kind; if my father hadn't been quite so gentle and kind. If my friends were only more supportive; if society hadn't demanded that women be married. If men weren't so arrogant; if my professors had taught me to think instead of requiring me to be a parrot. You get the idea.

At the same time, I believed it was really all *my* fault that my life wasn't working out. Even so, I kept doing the same things over and over, expecting different results. I was stuck.

It wasn't until I could see how I influenced the events and people in my life that I was able to make some genuine progress. And I couldn't see myself clearly enough to change as long as I believed that I was defective, worthless, unlovable, or as long as I continued to blame others, seeing myself as a victim of other people and circumstances.

I couldn't change my self-perception until I sought God's presence and began to trust in His love. I began to experience God's love directly through prayer and through the love of spiritual people He put into my life those who believed in me and accepted me no matter what. In the astounding presence of love, I began to take some risks and let myself be vulnerable to God and others.

Here are some of the things I found out about myself. I was possessive of my friends and dependent on their approval to be okay. I didn't like to share them with others. Many years ago, when I was a student in New York, I had several close girlfriends. We were all good friends, but I rarely went out with them as a group. It was always one at a time. When there was more than one, I began to feel left out, like a hole in a doughnut. I had to have my friend's complete attention so I could gauge her reactions and know that I existed.

I was dependent on others to tell me what to do so that if anything went wrong, I had someone to blame. I wanted to be able to scientifically behave, according to some formula, so that I wouldn't make mistakes. I tried to get Ruthie, my surrogate mom, to tell me exactly what to do to keep my latest love in my life or to make my boss appreciate me. You try having a relationship of any kind in this fashion and see how well it works! I guarantee you, it doesn't.

I didn't trust my own opinion or intuition so I looked to friends, co-workers, or supervisors for validation. Does this outfit look okay? Do I look fat? What did he mean when he said that? Do you think that's God's will? Should I go out with this guy? Do you like him? Did I sound okay at the staff meeting, or do you think my idea was dumb?

I was also angry a lot because other people didn't meet my expectations for how they should behave. Expectations are down payments on resentments. My mother didn't love me the way I thought she should. I was mad at her. My boss didn't give me the letter of commendation I thought I deserved. I was mad at him. My boyfriend didn't give me a present on my birthday, my co-worker wouldn't cover my shift, my friend betrayed a confidence. I would be mad at them, too. I became critical and judgmental of others, which, in turn, caused me to communicate in an abrasive, tactless, and hurtful manner. No one escaped my opinions, not my friends, family, colleagues, not even the poor waiter whose bad luck it was to be serving me in a restaurant.

Family and friends felt they needed to walk on eggshells around me since I was so easily hurt or upset. This led them to be dishonest with me, not wanting to say what they really felt. You can well imagine what my family thought about the wedding taking place in my sister's backyard. There I was, having been raised in a Jewish home and about to become a doctor, marrying Ali, my Muslim Iranian busboy (you remember—he was one of my false gods), in a ceremony that I had written, being performed by a hapless Unitarian Universalist minister who had no idea what he had gotten himself into. My family was there, their friends were there, my therapist was there, Ali's friends were there, and so were mine. No one dared to say what they really thought of this insane match!

People avoided me when I was in one of my moods. I would often hear my mother say to my dad, "Leave her alone. She'll get over it." Dad would put his arms around me and have a helpless look in his eyes while I sobbed over the latest tragedy in my life.

I was afraid of letting people see I was vulnerable or needy, so I sought to be in control. I maintained control by "helping" others, making them dependent on me. I'd been doing this since I was a child. I didn't believe anyone would like me just for me. But if I made myself indispensable by always being available to listen, comfort, or dispense advice, maybe they would accept me and stay around. I suppose that's when I first became a psychologist, but then it was for all the wrong reasons.

When you place yourself in the loving care of God and others who knowingly live in God's love, all your nasty, selfish, icky attitudes and shortcomings, which you have been trying so hard to avoid seeing, will rise to the surface. It is important to understand that pessimism, complaining, whining, ungratefulness, fear, anger, disappointment, and self-pity do not come from God. They come from ego, and remember, ego equals "edging God out."

If some person or situation disturbs you, and you find yourself experiencing any of those feelings or attitudes, it is because your ego feels threatened. It then serves up a thought, a feeling, or a character defect to defend you. The problem is that these defenses become habits that interfere with developing healthy relationships, attitudes, and life strategies. They push you into repeating old behaviors, which become the self-defeating patterns in your life. This is how you sabotage yourself and stay in self instead of resting in God.

When I first met Ruthie, who, as you might remember, later became my surrogate mom, I believed that my own mother was the cause of all my problems. My mother always told me, "Only the people who love you will tell you the truth." Then she would lay some truth on me, and I'd be out for the round. I felt terribly judged and criticized. I reacted with hurt and anger, developing a low opinion of myself. I became extremely needy of her approval. When I couldn't seem to get it no matter how hard I tried, I began to look for approval from everyone else in the universe, or so it seemed. If someone criticized me I got angry, not because the other person made me angry but because I was protecting the needy part of me that yearned for approval to prove I was an okay person. I could not accept anything less.

Ruthie became my loving guide. She helped me believe that God loved me and that I could also trust her love for me. Her love and God's love gave me the courage to look at the things in me that were opposite to God or love so that I could be healed.

When I could finally see how my attitudes and defensive or needy behaviors affected my relationships and self-esteem, I came to understand that I was the cause of the negative patterns in my life. This was a horrifying truth to swallow at first. I much preferred believing that my problems were my mother's or boyfriend's or boss's fault. But ultimately, this became the basis of true freedom. If I was the source of the problems in my life, I had the power to change so my life could be better.

How to Identify Defects of Character

Under the warmth of God's love and Ruthie's nurturing, I learned to take steps to discover the negative attitudes and defects—forms of self-centeredness—that kept me from the joy and peace and healthy relationships God meant me to have.

In this section are some steps that I've found helpful in discovering my own shortcomings. My approach to uncovering character defects resembles the method used in Twelve Step programs. If you've already done this kind of self-exploration, you might consider using the following suggestions as a tune-up. (See appendix 2: "Common Defects of Character" for additional help.)

- Ask God for help. Ask Him to put a loving spiritual friend, guide, or mentor in your life to help you to discover and be the person God already knows you are.
- Ask God to teach you by speaking through this other person and through your own heart, where the still small voice within—your intuition or the Spirit of God—resides.
  - Identify the feeling of anger or fear.
  - Write down what has happened to trigger the emotion.

- ◆ Figure out how the anger or fear affects your life.
- ◆ See what behavior results from these feelings—how you protect yourself.
- ◆ Look for defects of character or shortcomings that came into play, causing you to be angry, fearful, hurt, or anxious in the first place. (Remember, the other person or event didn't cause the disruption. It's your reaction that's the culprit.)
- ◆ Ask your spiritual guide to help you identify the character defects involved.
- ◆ Ask your loving God to remove these defects and help you replace the old patterns with new ones.

When you allow the traits that are opposite to love to become visible, love will heal them. Just ask God to take these things, and, at exactly the right pace for you, He will.

At this point, I hope that, like me at this stage, you'll find that you've begun to know yourself really well. I had begun to experience a taste of the true humility and comfort that came from seeing myself exactly as I am, with all my assets and limitations, and accepting myself. I am convinced that such self-knowledge and acceptance were made possible by my greater experience of God's love—a love that I believe extends to everyone. I had come to recognize God as a true friend as well as lover, and now I was beginning to desire to spend more and more time with Him.

Chapter 5

Hanging Out with God

The more I got to know God, the more I wanted to spend time with Him. It seemed that I couldn't get enough of Him. In the early years of our relationship, it appeared that God couldn't get enough of me.

My prayer life seemed blessed. I was entranced with God's presence in my life. Everything I asked for seemed to come my way. It was more like God was obedient to me than I was obedient to God. I had taken God hostage and wanted Him all to myself. I felt beautiful, intelligent, worthwhile, beloved, whole, and healed of all that had been wrong in my world. At last, I was getting my fix. The good thing was that it was from God rather than from men, success, or material things.

I suppose that God knew that this was the way it had to be with me. He had to gain my trust and build my strength so that I could weather the stormy seas that would come later on. I thrived in God's warmth, and I glowed in the reflection of His light.

Instead of going on vacations to beach resorts or the usual cultural meccas such as New York, Boston, London, or Paris, I went on retreats so that I could hang out with God. After my first weekend retreat, I upped the ante on intensity. Only three years into my relationship with God, I found myself on an eight-day retreat that, much to my surprise, was silent.

Silent?

I had never been silent in my life. If anything, I avoided being alone like the plague. I was fearful of my own thoughts and feelings.

What in the world am I doing here?

There I was, Queen of the Dire Need for Approval and Validation, on a silent retreat with twenty or thirty clergymen and women who didn't talk to me, look at me, or even smile or frown at me. Was I dressed right? Was I acting appropriately? Was I praying correctly? I had no idea.

The only person I spoke to was my assigned individual retreat director, and, of course, I talked to God. Elizabeth was a warm and wonderful woman who would soon be ordained as an Episcopal priest. We met each day for about forty-five minutes. She explained that the real director of the retreat was the Holy Spirit, God within me. She was just there to help me discern the direction in which God appeared to be leading me and to validate my experience. She suggested scripture and other spiritual readings, and she instructed me to spend four separate hours each day just being with God in prayer.

What on earth did that mean? What were God and I to do or talk about for four hours? Using my imagination, I was to enter into the Bible scenes I was reading and take part in the events or conversations that were being depicted. Or I could imagine talking over spiritual readings with God, letting the Spirit guide me to understanding. It all sounded pretty nuts to me!

I was going stir-crazy by the middle of the second day, and I was seriously considering getting out of there before I was carried out in a straitjacket. So I told God, "God, I am about to blow this joint. Maybe the only reason I am here is to find out that this is not for me. So, if You want me to stay, You had better do something quickly to change my mind."

Within minutes, I found myself heading toward the stream. When I got there, it had become the River Jordan in my imagination, and I could see Jesus being baptized by John. Suddenly, I was wading into the river so that I could be baptized by John. It was amazingly real to me.

After that, I was off and running for the rest of the week. I was a child being taken to temple by Joseph and Mary. I picnicked on the mount with Jesus. I was Peter denying that I knew Jesus. I was Veronica offering my scarf to wipe Jesus' brow. I was at the foot of the cross with the women who were closest to Him. And I was on the road to Emmaus being taught by Him.

By the end of the retreat, I not only knew my God better, but I also knew above all and absolutely that I was never alone. God was with me, not only when I prayed, but also when I ate, when I slept, when I worked, when I played, and even in the shower.

Right Thoughts, Right Words, Right Actions, and Right Attitudes, or There Is Nothing That God and I Can't Handle Together

I'm a night person. So I end my day in prayer. In this way, I can review the past twenty-four hours and prepare for the coming day. When I go to bed, I want to know that my thoughts, words, actions, and attitudes were satisfactory not only in my own eyes but also in God's eyes. If this was the case, my day was a success. When I have remembered to spend time with God throughout the day, I have a good shot at feeling comfortable about how it went.

Some days, I'm my own boss. God isn't at the steering wheel. In fact, he isn't even in the car with me. On these days, I wake up thinking I don't want to get up. Then I realize I'm already running late. Oh brother, I have a million patients today. I'm going to get to work late. I won't catch up until halfway through lunch. Then there won't be any time to relax and eat.

When I finally get to the office, I remember the report I was going to write during my lunchtime. Then my secretary reminds me that I have phone calls I have to make right away.

By afternoon, I'm distracted and irritable, my spirits are low, and I'm tired. Time for more coffee so that I don't nod off while a patient is talking. I think I'll scream if I have to listen to any whining or if anyone is too needy. I'm abrupt with the people who have come to me for help, and I feel annoyed with myself.

Dinnertime is spent writing the report I should have written hours ago. I'm stressed so it's hard to focus on the task at hand.

I end up writing the report after I've seen ten or twelve patients so I don't do the job as well as I wanted to.

I get home late, almost too tired to pray. But I do, no matter what. As a result, I can see where I've failed, especially in living my life today as if God didn't exist. My thoughts, words, actions, and attitudes have hurt others who have crossed my path. And I've been uptight, anxious, and generally miserable all day. This is no way to live. So I ask God to help me do better tomorrow, and I know He will, if I let Him.

Don't Step on the Hose

I have often sabotaged my prayer life by stepping on the hose, cutting off the flow of the Spirit. I had an all-or-nothing attitude for a long time. If I couldn't feel successful at prayer, I just wouldn't pray. What did I mean by success? To me, it meant having strong feelings and being deeply emotional. Not wanting to wait for the bidding of God, I tried to control my prayer life. I wanted to make prayer happen in my own time and in my own way instead of in God's way and time.

For the first six years of my new relationship with God, I was a single woman, unencumbered by responsibilities outside of work. My life was my own. I went where I wanted to go when I wanted to go. I did what I wanted to do. I prayed uninterrupted when I wanted to pray. If I wanted silence, I had silence. If I wanted to go away on an eight-day retreat, I went.

Under these conditions, it was easy to hang out with God. It was fun. My prayer seemed very fruitful, and I enjoyed my time with God. Even when I was feeling sad, angry, remorseful, helpless, confused, or any other emotion that people classify as negative, I enjoyed my prayer. That is because I felt connected to God. I was talking to my best friend and lover. I liked to talk about my difficulties, as most women do, and I felt the burden lessen as I shared with God.

Then my life changed. My mother died, and my father was lost in his sadness. I soon found out that he was in the early stages of vascular dementia, caused by diabetes and ministrokes. I became a mother, and four months later, my dad moved in with me and my newborn daughter. My life now seemed cluttered, noisy, busy. My time was no longer my own. I had other people who depended on me for attention. Not surprisingly, I began to have trouble with prayer. I didn't have time to pray. I kept getting interrupted. When I tried to pray, I got distracted. I couldn't focus. I started to rely more on other people to tell me what to do and consulted less with God. Or worse, I kept everything to myself, not letting anyone in. I have to tell you that the self consulting the self about the self is an exercise doomed to failure!

During the next seven years, I felt worse and worse about myself because I could see my shortcomings reflected in my dad's or daughter's eyes when I was acting like a jerk. I discovered that it's easy to be a saint when you live alone with two cats. But when I got knee deep in the flow of life, I got lost. I was stepping on the hose, blocking God's good.

People often put a crimp in God's work with avoidance thinking:

1. I don't have time. I'm too busy.
2. What's the point? I keep getting interrupted.
3. I can't focus. Nothing is happening. I'm bored.
4. I'm too tired, too busy, too overwhelmed. I'm too stressed, too depressed, too . . .
5. I don't know how to pray, or I'm not doing it right.
6. It's too painful. I don't like the truth that gets revealed.
7. I'm too emotional. I can't tell God how I really feel.
8. I'm angry at God, and it's totally unacceptable to express how unhappy I am with Him.
9. I'm too sinful. I can't talk to God until I've cleaned up my act.
10. I can't pray for myself because that's selfish. I don't know what's okay to pray about.
11. I'm afraid of what God will want from me.

To open the flow of God's gracious good will, start right where you are. The best place to begin your prayer is with any of the "reasons" (excuses?) you have for not praying. If you put

God in charge of your prayer life, He'll provide the answers you need.

How to Hang Out with God through Prayer

I was able to take the style of prayer that I learned on retreat into my daily prayer life. It's certainly not the only style of prayer, but it suited me perfectly. Each person must find the way best suited to his or her own personality or temperament. Ask your God to lead you to the way of prayer best suited to you. Before you know it, you'll be transported into a new and deeper relationship with God—one better than you ever could have imagined.

There are many ways to pray. There's no right or wrong about which method you choose, but the chosen style should be authentic for you. What is important is that you do pray, because spending time or hanging out with God is the path to building a relationship with Him.

People are often at a loss as to how to get started in prayer. Here are some suggestions for beginners:

1. Make a decision to take action and try to pray, even if you feel foolish, uncertain, afraid of making a mistake, or bashful about meeting God.

2. Tell God that you want to know Him better and that you want Him to know you. I believe God desires to be in a relationship with us far more than we will ever want to be in one with Him. God is very patient. He'll wait for us however long it takes and He won't force Himself on us.

3. Schedule a regular time for daily prayer. It doesn't matter where you choose to pray or what position you assume for prayer. It's helpful to pick a place where you can feel comfortable and secure, but if such a spot is not available to you, don't allow that fact to deter you. If necessary, pray in the car, behind a closed door at the office, on a lunchtime walk, in the bathtub. Just pray!

4. Share with God your problems, wishes, desires, hopes, dreams, fears. Tell God about decisions you need to make

or confusion you have. Talk to God as you would to a best friend.

5. Read something spiritual or religious—the Bible, a daily devotional book, a sacred book from your particular spiritual path or religion, or one of the thousands of books written about God or living a godly way of life. After reading, spend some time thinking about what you have read. Write down some of the insights or thoughts you had about the chosen passage or devotion. Talk about the reading with others during the day. Your thoughts and others' reactions are probably God's way of talking to you.

6. Listen to beautiful, spiritual music; gaze at inspirational art; take a walk in nature and pay close attention to the wonders evident in its majesty as well as in the smallest things; garden or work the soil; create music, art, or poetry. Recognize God in all these things.

7. Thank God for everything: love, joy, beauty, inspiration, as well as the difficult and painful feelings and events in your life through which you will undoubtedly grow, season, and improve.

8. Participate in communal prayer in your house of worship, prayer group, support group, or Bible (or other scripture) study. Repeat spiritual phrases or prayers, sing hymns, or gaze at symbols that remind you of your God.

9. Review your day before you go to sleep. Thank God for the things you've done well and ask for help in the areas where you may need to improve—actions, attitudes, harmful habits.

As you progress in your prayer life, you may want to adopt prayer approaches that will draw you even deeper into the mystery of God, His world, and His love. There are many ways to do this, all of them equally good. The challenge is to find the method that works for you. Here are just a few of them:

- **Ignatian Prayer:** Ignatius Loyola was a sixteenth century soldier until he was seriously injured. He was called into a life of prayer and spent several months alone in a cave.

During that time, he had mystical experiences leading to the development of *The Spiritual Exercises of Saint Ignatius* and the Ignatian method of prayer. This is the approach to prayer that I learned during my silent retreat. Using your imagination, place yourself in a scene from the scripture or sacred text of your faith. See yourself as one of the characters or as part of the crowd. Interact or dialogue with others in the story and find out what they have to tell you. I often imagine myself sitting down for a meal or driving in my car with Jesus, or sitting in the palm of God's hand. You can imagine yourself with the spiritual guide or ideal that has meaning to you. Then have a conversation with God, both speaking and listening. Savor the closeness.

- **Visualization:** Any image held firmly in the mind over a long enough period of time will eventually become part of the unconscious. Reinforced by prayer, the imagined goal becomes belief, and when you pray believing, it will become reality. See in your mind's eye outcomes or accomplishments you would like to achieve. Imagine yourself being kind and tolerant to someone you can't stand. See yourself calmly taking a test or being confident during an interview. Visualize a full bank account, bills paid, working at a new job. Imagine yourself turning down that extra bite of food, refusing the drink or smoke that's just been offered. Make a collage of the way you'd like your life to look in three months or a year, and look at the collage each day. Write an affirmation that reflects your visualization. Know that any success you achieve is a gift from God.

- *Lectio Divina:* This method of prayer is divided into three stages. *Lectio* involves reading a passage from a familiar spiritual book, such as the Bible, until a sentence or phrase or word catches your attention in some deeply felt way. In *Meditatio,* you repeatedly say, sing, or chant the sentence or phrase that caught your attention. Keep varying where you put the emphasis until you feel the words become a deep part of you. The final stage is *Oratio.* When you are ready, stop chanting, become silent, and try to understand what the words or phrases mean to you. How do they speak to you? Listen. When answers come, they may engender more questions. Listen again. The answers come from the "still small voice within," the gentle whispering of the Spirit.

- **Fasting:** Fasting is most commonly associated with giving up all food or a particular kind of food for a period of time. This is often prescribed by a formal religious tradition. Catholics do not eat meat on Ash Wednesday or Good Friday, and they might forgo a particular food or beverage throughout Lent. Other religious traditions call upon their followers to give up all food during a prescribed period of time. In Jewish tradition, fasting is done communally on the holiest day of the year, Yom Kippur, the Day of Atonement. On this day, Jews pray for individual and communal forgiveness. It is a day on which amends may be made. In Christian tradition, fasting is a way of identifying with and sharing in the experience of Jesus spending forty days in the wilderness fasting and resisting the temptations of the devil. Jesus teaches that fasting strengthens our resolve to do right. Fasting may also commemorate special feast days or holy days such as Good Friday or the days of Ramadan in the Muslim tradition. Individuals may make a choice to fast from time to time. Fasting is a way to acknowledge God. It helps us to remember the gifts that God has given us, to recognize our fragility and need for His strength, to turn our focus inward to find our shortcomings, and to ask for God's help in routing them out. Fasting does not have to be restriction of food. It can also involve the resolve to fast from negative or harmful attitudes or behaviors or to go out of our way to do good works (fasting from selfishness).

- **Prayer of Forgiveness:** If there's any one thing that can block your good, it's a failure to forgive or show mercy—nursing a desire for revenge or holding a grudge. As long as you remain angry, you give the person or thing you're angry at rent-free space in your head. Anger drains your energy and blocks your ability to love or have peace. In its most virulent form, it becomes an obsession, a false god. The person or thing you can't forgive has control over you, and God can't get in. So forgiving is critical for your well-being. It's of utmost importance to know that forgiving someone doesn't condone the other's behavior. It doesn't relieve the other of responsibility for the wrong done. It simply and mightily allows God to be the judge, the jury, and the executioner so that you can go on with your life. A powerful way to pray to forgive another is to ask God to give the person with whom you are angry all the blessings in life you want for yourself—health, happiness, peace, joy, prosperity. Do this every day for at least two weeks and you'll find sunlight starting to chase the darkness. Each time you have an angry thought about the person, ask God to save you from being angry and lead you to better things. You don't have to mean it when you pray it. The willingness provides the necessary start, and God will take care of the rest.

- **Metaphysical or Scientific Prayer:** The emphasis in this form of prayer is on changing your mind. Problems become deeply rooted in thought, and negative thought produces like emotions. So if you are caught up in "what if" thoughts, feelings of fear will soon follow. If you are focused on lack in your life, financial fear will overwhelm you. Or, if you are concentrating on another's mistreatment of you, anger will express itself. Whatever thoughts and emotions you have will then become manifest in your life as an outcome. Financial fear becomes real financial difficulty. Health worries result in sickness. Anger results in relationship difficulties, and so on. Metaphysical prayer teaches you to focus on the Spirit of God within, focusing the mind away from the problem and onto the solution, which is God. (Remember Spiritual Drano from chapter 1?) Raise your consciousness to God through prayer, repeating spiritual affirmations, reading spiritual literature, and basically going on a mental diet from all negative thinking. By unit-

ing with God-consciousness, your problems will be solved
and good will manifest in your life.

- **Centering Prayer:** Practicing centering prayer means
  emptying your mind of internal thoughts and feelings,
  letting go of the stresses and challenges of your external
  life and becoming still. Like all other forms of prayer, this
  requires practice and gentle patience with yourself. You
  might try to imagine clouds passing by and placing your
  random thoughts or feelings on the cloud, watching them
  pass out of sight. Or watch your thoughts floating down
  a river while you sit on the riverbank. Pick a sacred word,
  and when you notice thoughts, emotions, body sensa-
  tions, or external sounds, say the chosen word to bring
  you back to awareness of God's presence within. After a
  period of time, twenty or thirty minutes, begin to have a
  conversation with God or go back to your usual thoughts.
  Listen for God throughout the day. He will speak to you
  in your thoughts, through other people, through events of
  the day.

These are only brief descriptions of several methods of prayer.
There are many books written that teach them in greater detail.
There are also many other ways to pray. The important thing to
remember is that when you pray, you are hanging out with God,
deepening your relationship with Him, and opening the channel
to become all that God wants you to be.

As you become more comfortable with one or more of these
methods of prayer, you'll find your relationship with God changing. Instead of a one-way street with you doing all the talking,
you will become a holy listener. Now your relationship with God
will be more mutual and more satisfying. And this greater depth
of relationship will make you long to spend even more time with
God and deepen your desire to please Him. You are ready for a
stronger commitment and willing to consider doing God's will,
whatever in the world that may be.

Chapter 6

Doing God's Will

*A*s I grew closer to God and I knew more about Him, I began to realize that it wasn't just me growing closer to God. He also wanted to be closer to me.

I believed it when I read that God has a plan for me which is for good, not for evil. The thing is that His plan unfolds slowly as I learn more about God's will for me and try to act on it.

Now this idea of doing God's will was a new one. *What does this mean? How do I learn about it? What is required?* It sounded exciting when I thought about all the goodies I imagined God had in store for me. It also seemed scary. *What if I didn't like God's plan? What if God wanted more of me than I really wanted to give?*

I was very mixed up about this. On the one hand, I couldn't imagine people wanting to hold back part of themselves from God. On the other hand, if I were truly honest with myself, maybe I would want to reserve judgment and take a wait-and-see attitude. Maybe I wanted to be in charge of my financial life and spend my money however I felt like spending it. Perhaps I wasn't ready to give God power over what I ate and whether I exercised. It could be that self-righteous anger along with being judgmental and intolerant were useful traits on occasion. Sometimes it felt good to be childish and stubborn or dependent and irresponsible.

Surely God wouldn't want me to give up everything, including my guilty delights. ALL OF ME? Don't I need some autonomy? Can't I hold back just a little?

Of course. I can hold back or give up as much or as little as I want.

God is patient. He wants to give Himself totally, but He waits until I'm ready. Each time I give up a little more of myself to God, I make a little more room for Him to shape me and my life according to His wonderful but secret and mysterious plan.

When I was in the navy, I met a young physician who told me that he'd been deeply affected by the story of Francis of Assisi. Francis was a wealthy young man in the early thirteenth century when he asked God to remove any attachments he had to anything other than God. Called to live a simple life, he and his followers gave away all their worldly goods and traveled around the country teaching people about God's love.

This doctor was so inspired by Francis's story that he closed his budding private practice. He gave up his possessions and went to practice medicine among the poor. He not only felt guided by God but also liberated by this decision.

Soon after meeting that doctor, I heard a woman tell how she'd prayed to God to remove her dependence on anything or anyone other than Him. Not long after that, she lost her home during an earthquake, and her husband became ill, close to death. Through these difficult times, she felt that the only strength she had was her faith that God had a plan for her and that He would help her through. Her prayers were answered, and she had only God upon whom to depend. He turned out to be more than enough.

These two people inspired me. I asked God to remove any attachments I had to anyone or anything but Him. I did this by praying the prayer of the Jesuits that asks God, "Take all of me. Take my liberty, my memory, and my understanding. All that I am and all that I have has been given to me by You, God. I give it all back to You, knowing that Your love and Your grace are enough for me."

How's that for courage? Or was it total stupidity?

Don't Outline for God

About five years into my relationship with God, I went on one of my eight-day retreat vacations. Several days into this retreat, I began to wonder (for maybe the bazillionth time) where I fit in the universe. I wasn't married. I wasn't a clergyperson, and I wasn't a nun. The only identity that I seemed to have at the time was that of a naval officer. I wore the uniform, and I was assigned my job by a higher authority, the Naval Medical Command. In this context, I functioned as a psychologist and administrator. It didn't seem to be enough.

I began praying about this, and at some point during the retreat, I realized that the navy could be God's channel to send me places in the world where I would be able to be of greatest service to Him. My work as a psychologist, and especially my expertise working with alcoholics and addicts, could be my ministry.

I believed with all my heart that this was God's will for me. After all, this idea came to me while I was seriously meditating on God's Word. So, with a passion, I threw myself into doing the footwork to make this happen. I would be like a nun in a navy uniform! Just think how many sailors would get sober and stay that way once they met God through my exalted spiritual channel and had recovery explained to them through my anointed psychological insights. I had found my place in the universe.

When I returned to work after this retreat with God, I called the navy's chief psychologist to tell him that I wanted orders to the U.S. Naval Hospital in Japan where I could be the director of the Alcohol Rehabilitation Service. It seemed to me that there I could best fulfill God's plans for me, since I could help not only the sailors who were sent to treatment but also all the English-speaking civilians who would need my help in getting sober. The psychologist in charge of placing us told me he could probably make my transfer to Japan happen once I got promoted to lieutenant commander. So I became obsessed with promotion. After all, I was on a mission from God!

Because psychologists in the navy were also expected to be hospital administrators, I went back to school at night to get a master's degree in health services management. I needed another degree like I needed a hole in the head, but if that would help me carry out what I was convinced was God's will, so be it. I took on difficult and time-consuming collateral duties at the hospital. These earned me a Navy Achievement Medal and a trip to the hospital with IV steroid treatment for stress-related rashes.

I was so busy preparing myself to be of service to God when I eventually got to Japan that I was of little earthly good to anyone who crossed my path in the meantime. I was busy and on the run, accomplishing important things, right?

I had no time for my friends, but they would understand, wouldn't they? I had to be at work extra hours, since I had become the command physical fitness coordinator, and measuring some overweight sailor's waist was critical to my promotion plan. So when a friend was having difficulty and needed my understanding ear, it was nowhere to be found. I was putting together an original quality assurance program, hoping for medal recognition, which would be good for promotion. Co-workers who needed to consult with me about a difficult patient would surely forgive me for being too distracted to pay close attention. A command party was politically important for that promotion. Unfortunately, I just couldn't fulfill that other commitment I had made. All for a good reason, of course. My efforts paid off. I managed to get my orders to Japan even before the promotion board met, so sure was I and everyone else that I would get promoted. I thought I was doing the footwork to achieve promotion and leaving the results to God. But the fact was that, while I was sure I was doing God's will, I was unknowingly running on extreme self-will and getting ready to crash.

The navy promotion board met, and I was passed over for promotion. As a result, my orders for Japan were canceled.

But did I surrender? Of course not! I still believed that a career in the navy was God's will for me.

I redoubled my efforts during the next year. I passed my licensing exams, and I knew this would be my ticket to ride. The promotion board met again, and I was passed over again. That meant that I had to get out of the navy in six months' time. Basically, I was fired! How could this be? I felt tricked and deceived by God. What was the point of trusting Him if He only let me down? I was angry and depressed. It took several months to get up and get moving, looking for a new job, a new path.

It seemed that God had other plans for me. I had always said, "Let your will, not mine, be done." I believed with all my heart that I meant it. But when it turned out that God's will was not the same as mine, I was angry and devastated.

It seems that I had conditions on accepting God's plan. I still had an important lesson to learn: Don't outline for God!

The Sound of God's Will

How do I know if I am doing God's will? I mean, He's not standing here in front of me, hands on hips, shaking His divine forefinger and saying, "You'd better do it this way, Judith, or you'll be sorry!" There are no Goodyear blimps with LED lights or beach planes leaving smoke trails saying, "Attention, Judith! God's will is as follows . . ." There are no notes from God left in my lunch cooler. Answers in the Magic 8-Ball leave a lot to be desired. And if I play Scripture Roulette, where I ask a question and open the Bible (or another spiritual book) at random, I might get an answer, but I am more likely than not to end up even more confused than before.

This is where I think the right use of guilt comes in. God planted this particular stop sign right in our gut to let us know that we're about to screw up or, worse, that we've already made a royal mess. I just hurt someone's feelings. Just spent money I didn't have on something I didn't need. Just lied to avoid trouble or disapproval. Just broke a promise to myself, to someone else, or to God.

The whole purpose of guilt is to let us know we are about to step or have already stepped outside of our value system or moral code. We have sinned in the sense of damaging the relationship with ourselves, with another person, or with the Divine.

It seems highly unlikely that behavior reflecting God's will for me would cause me to feel guilt. In fact, once the red light flashes informing me that I've done wrong, guilt has served its purpose. It's probably not God's will for me to hold onto guilt and keep beating myself up. That only leaves me broken and doesn't fix anything. Instead, it seems to me that God will be pleased if I ask for the forgiveness that He generously gives, make amends for harm done in whatever way seems appropriate, and try my best to do better. When I have done these things, I am likely to feel peace, which is always a gift from God.

Choosing a right course of action is for me the trickier part of knowing God's will. Do I pay for repairs on my car, which has

150,000 miles on it and which I drive 100 miles a day over rough terrain, or do I buy a new one? Do I accept a new job that has been offered to me, or do I go for the promotion that's opening up at my current job? Should I call this man or wait for him to call me? Should I stay at a hotel the night before the seminar or drive 90 miles in the morning to save money? On and on the questions go, about all kinds of things, small and large, momentous and trivial.

What I do know is that I can't always see exactly what God's will is. I'm convinced that my desire to live God's way pleases Him. Experience has shown me that if I offer myself to God each day and ask for His guidance, He'll give it. It will come to me through my intuition (gut feeling, still small voice within), through something I read, or through a remark that a friend makes. It will come through a seeming coincidence or a chance meeting. If I am alert and listening, it will come.

If I'm sincere about my desire to please God, He won't let me stray far. I believe that God keeps me on an extremely long leash. He gives me room to move around and make my own decisions. If I wander too far and begin to fall dangerously off the palm of God's very large hand, He gives the leash a gentle but firm yank and gets me back on course. When the decision is a large one, not only do I pray for guidance, but I also discuss it with one or two trusted friends. I resist shopping for an opinion that matches what I want to hear. If I mess up, I get to learn from my mistakes.

Ultimately, if I'm in God's will, I'll feel peace. As a Jesuit priest explained to me, "The sound of self-will is like the sound of water crashing on a rock, but the sound of God's will is like the sound of water dripping on a sponge." My heart and my gut are made to know the difference.

God Has Just Three Answers:
"Yes," "No," and "Not Now"

One day, a little boy's favorite ball slipped out of his hands and went rolling into the street. He went running after the ball, not seeing a car racing toward him. The boy's father ran to him, scooped him up, and carried him to safety a moment before the car would have hit him. The car missed the boy but crushed the ball.

Often we are chasing after one of our "favorite balls," but God is like a loving father who sees the whole picture. He rescues us, just in the nick of time, before we get run over by one of our seemingly brilliant, but actually bad, decisions. It doesn't feel like we've been saved. Until we have the perspective of time, it seems like painful loss.

As a child, I felt drawn toward the Catholic faith. When I began to get to know God as an adult, I asked the hunky navy chaplain priest to instruct me in the faith. He agreed, but he said that he would not baptize me unless he believed that I was ready and that my conversion was sincere.

"Sure," I said. "No problem. I understand."

We set a date for the big day, but several weeks prior, he said I wasn't ready. I was devastated and heartbroken. I felt God himself was rejecting me. And once again, I felt worthless and unloved. I didn't understand.

This wonderful man kept instructing me and helping me to grow spiritually—in spite of myself, I might add. Though he was a priest and my teacher, I also thought I was quite in love with him. Remember, to me, all men were gods! And he was no exception. God, however, was like a wise parent when he told me through this priest, "Not now!"

Shortly after that, my beloved spiritual guide received orders for overseas duty. I was heartbroken again.

A new chaplain arrived in my teacher's place, but I wasn't open to him. I think I felt something like what Jesus' disciples must have felt when he told them he was going away but he would send them a "comforter" who would bring them peace. Who wanted a new comforter? I was in mourning for my friend, who had been ordered away.

After a while, I came to realize that my first instructor had become a god to me. When he went away, I had to decide whether it was him that I wanted or God.

Slowly, I realized that my comfort came from talking to God, talking about God, and from listening to God through prayer, spiritual reading, and hearing His message at church. I allowed the new chaplain to be God's new voice in my life and to teach me. Eventually, I was baptized. While I waited, I had grown and matured in my faith. I realized that God's apparent "no" was actually a "not now." In the end, this spiritual event was far more meaningful to me on God's time than it would have been if I'd been baptized in my time. God had waited for me to be ready to receive this gift before He said "yes."

. . .

I have been in my own private practice for the past sixteen years. At times I get really burned out with what I'm doing. I'm tired of going to my office. Everything about it annoys or stresses me. My patients are particularly troubled, depressed, or even suicidal. There are seemingly constant emergencies, no one wants to take direction, everyone is whining or needy. By the end of the day, I feel like I need an IV to replace the nutrients that have been sucked out of me. It's not just the patients; it's also the secretary, the daily long-distance ride, the worry about taxes and retirement.

For three years, I had relied on Becky, my wonderful secretary, for everything. She had a big personality: friendly, honest, loyal, outspoken, funny. We were a great team. She had run the office smoothly, communicated well with my patients, dealt with insurance companies that were refusing authorizations for treatment or payment, reminded me of things that needed to be done, and perhaps, most important, she was a supportive friend. Wonderfully for her, and alas for me, she was accepted into nursing school, which she had been preparing for the whole time she'd worked for me. That was five years ago.

I went through two secretaries in the year after Becky left, and was starting on the third. I began to crave change for a variety of reasons, and I asked God for guidance.

Everything in my work life seemed a hassle, problematic, or unfulfilling. And there was no one around to listen to me whine. Gas prices were rising, and I was traveling a hundred miles every day. The freeway I took included a steep pass that is often its own weather zone, with fog, sleet, and rain, as well as fires and chemical spills from train wrecks.

I wanted greater security, including health and retirement benefits along with sick and vacation days. I was fed up with the high cost of individual health care. I was tired of dealing with the hassle of paying quarterly self-employment and payroll taxes. Frankly, I never wanted to hire or fire another person.

On top of everything else, my office looked like a disaster area. It badly needed redecorating, painting, and renovating, and the landlord was unwilling to provide any service toward this end.

I was lonely and felt this more acutely after Becky left. I thought having some colleagues around to hang out with and to talk with about patients and clinical issues might be just the ticket.I began to look for work close to home. First, I applied for a position working for the Vet Center, helping veterans suffering from post-traumatic stress disorder and their families. The job had been posted by the VA on several prior occasions without being filled. I was highly qualified, and I almost superstitiously believed that it had reopened at this moment in time just for me. It must be God's will, right? Wrong! I was not hired; the job went to someone else.

Next, I applied at a state hospital near my home. A close friend of mine had been a chaplain there for many years. He encouraged me, even though I wasn't thrilled about working at a mental hospital treating the criminally insane. I went to the hospital with my application and was fortunate to catch the chief psychologist in his office. He knew my chaplain friend and was enthusiastic about my applying to become a psychologist there, not only because of my experience but also because of the great need for additional staff.

Apparently, the Department of Justice had just completed a review stating that the staff/patient ratio was too low. Positions needed to be filled, and quickly. Here I was at just the right moment in time, right? Wrong. It seemed that the state credentialing committee required that the Ph.D. be in clinical psychology, not counseling psych, as mine was. I know of no other institution that made such a differentiation, but the desperate state apparently did.

Two "no's" from God so far. The chief psychologist said that if I wanted to go ahead and apply, he would see if he could obtain an exception from the credentialing committee. But I had learned the hard way, through my navy experience, that when something is God's will, the doors open with ease. No doors were opening here. This was a repeat-for-correction, and I had learned my lesson.

My next attempt at change was to apply to a behavioral medicine group near my home. The man who did my medical billing also provided services for this group, and he spoke highly of the psychiatrist who owned it. The group needed another psychologist on staff at the time that I was applying at the Vet Center, and the owner seemed to be interested in my joining. This would be a shoo-in, right? Wrong! By the time I finished applying for the state hospital position, the spot at the behavioral medicine group was filled.

At this point, I gave up looking for a job with benefits or one that was close to home. But maybe it would be enough to have colleagues and shared responsibility for staff hiring and firing. I began talking to three other clinicians who practiced in the same city as I did and who were interested in joining together to form a group. We were quite excited at the prospect. This should surely work out, right? Wrong! As it turned out, one of the three was going to be moving out of town in a year, and we couldn't find adequate office space in the city where we were already established.

So what's the deal, God? Do you want me to stay in my rundown office, far from home, with rising gas prices, with no benefits, hiring and firing my own secretaries, with no colleagues, doing the same old thing? I heard your four "no" answers loud and clear. Is this supposed to be a "not now"?

I had been praying for guidance, visualizing changes, keeping a positive attitude, and affirming God-centered outcomes. Was I doing something wrong? What lessons were there for me to learn?

I phoned my wise and loving friend Joannie. I had watched her go through many changes, running into apparent dead ends only to find out that they were necessary stepping-stones toward finding her right place.

She had wanted to leave California and find a position in her area of expertise. She was offered an opportunity to do just that, but as soon as she arrived in the new city, the position dissolved.

Joannie began working at an unrelated job just to keep a roof over her head. Though scared and disappointed, she turned to prayer, having faith that God had a plan for her. She kept interviewing, being open to moving again or even to doing something different from what she'd originally planned. Willing to be surprised by God, she wasn't disappointed. Joannie was offered a research and development position and has become a respected leader in her industry.

Joannie misses her friends in California and also the weather, the beach, and the cultural activities. God isn't done with her yet. More change could be in the wind. She just continues to do footwork, leaving the results to God.

I asked Joannie if she thought I was doing something wrong. She laughed heartily, saying she doubted that I was. Then, more seriously, she asked, "Are you asking God for things that are close to your heart?"

"What in the world are you talking about?" I was annoyed. This seemed like obvious evasiveness.

"Just what I said, Judith." Joannie went on to say, "There's nothing wrong with what you've been looking for. But is it really what you want? Are the changes you've been pursuing close to your heart? I mean—why would God want you to exchange your successful private practice for a new situation that won't make you happy or fulfilled?"

Now I was getting really ticked, and defensive. "It's not that I would especially love to do any of those things," I grudgingly admitted. "It's just that they seem practical and realistic, all things considered."

God often talks to us through other people, and that day God went by the name of Joannie.

"Judith," she said, with tender care, "for as long as I've known you—some six years now—you've always talked about wanting to do two things, write a book and lead retreats. Maybe it's time to follow your dreams."

That was all I needed to hear. The pieces fell into place.

Within a couple of weeks, I enrolled in a class called Introduction to Creative Nonfiction at the University of California,

Riverside Extension Center. Not long after the class started, I knew what I wanted to write.

Next, I took a look at my decrepit office. The words of my surrogate mom and mentor, who had died several years before, remained with me.

Ruthie had often told me, "As go the outsides, so go the insides."

No wonder I always felt in a hurry to get out of there. I made up my mind to redecorate and renovate. Forget the landlord. There was an unused group room that I could now visualize as a peaceful spot for spiritually oriented day retreats.

Two months later, I had an office that was comfortable and inviting. I had started writing this book about developing a relationship with God and achieving personal growth and fulfillment as a direct result. I was planning retreats focused on healing spiritual wounds, including hurt relationships with God, finding forgiveness for the unforgivable, and finding wholeness through the writing of spiritual autobiographies. As a result of the fulfillment I felt in these new undertakings, I found a renewed commitment and peace about my patients and day-to-day practice.

• • •

Here are some guidelines to help you figure out which answer you're getting from God:

1. Ask God for guidance. Tell God what you want, but be ready to accept His will if His answer is different. Remember that if you outline for God, you must resist getting attached to the outcome.
2. Do the footwork. To discern God's will, pray, take action, and thank God in advance for prayers answered. Apply for the job. Fill in the mortgage application. Talk over your proposed plans with someone who understands your desire to live a God-centered life. In other words, don't just sit and wait for discernment. Gather information and take what action you can in the meantime.
3. Pay attention to your intuition, the still small voice within. This is the Spirit talking. If your gut is in an uproar, pay at-

tention. If your thoughts sound like water crashing on a rock, take note. You have likely stepped out of God's will, and you are hearing a "no."

4. If the doors close, or you find yourself coming up against one barrier after another, the answer may be "no."

5. If a trusted friend who generally gives good advice and understands you seems doubtful about your course of action, God might be speaking through your friend and saying "no."

6. If you become obsessed with a particular course of action or an outcome and you can only hear your own thoughts, you might be caught up in self-will. That is a good time to say to yourself, "Not now." God is not in the obsession.

7. Any "no" can actually be a "not now," especially if there are lessons for you to learn before you get to "yes." This is often true when there is a repeat-for-correction in progress.

8. When all the doors open, when a path seems direct and clear, when the choice doesn't conflict with your moral or spiritual code, when your friends who love you are glad for you, and when your gut feels calm and your thoughts have the quiet sound of water dripping on a sponge, then God is probably saying "yes."

Always have faith that God has a plan for you and that it's for good. God wants you to have a good life. He's your wise and good and powerful provider, and He loves you with a love that has no end.

How to Recognize God's Will

Fifteen years ago, I met a pastor who had grown up wanting to be an air force pilot. When he applied for a commission, he was told that he had some visual problems that disqualified him. He was very disappointed. After a time, he decided to go to graduate school, but he wasn't accepted into any of the programs that he had applied to. So he decided to travel for awhile.

On his way, the future Pastor Brian met many people, and he found that he loved listening to them. He discovered that he had the ability to help others, and he made some deep friendships along the way. He also found himself increasingly connected with God as he saw more of the country. At some point, he realized that he had a desire to be ordained. However, given his past experience with career plans, he had some strong misgivings, fearing another rejection. Nevertheless, he applied to a Lutheran college, and, to his surprise, he was accepted quickly and received a stipend. The rest is history. He met no serious obstacles to achieving this goal.

In reflecting on the false starts he'd experienced on his career path, Brian remembered some loggers he'd met on his travels in Oregon. While observing them splitting wood for a campfire, it seemed to him that when a man struck a log in just the right place, it fell apart with ease. When the correct spot was missed, the men could hack away at the piece of wood, but it wouldn't split cleanly. It occurred to him that discerning God's will in his life was much the same as splitting wood. When something was God's will, the doors seem to fly open with ease. When it wasn't, Brian could chop and chop, trying to split the wood or open the door, and it simply wouldn't happen.

Pastor Brian shared this story with me after I told him that I was still struggling to understand what had happened to me when I was in the U.S. Navy. When I joined the navy as a psychologist, I was commissioned as an officer in the active reserves. This is like being a teacher without tenure. I was guaranteed employment as a naval officer psychologist for the length of my contract, which was initially for three years. If I wanted to stay in the navy until retirement, I had to be augmented, the equivalent of being tenured, into the regular navy.

To achieve augmentation, the candidate undergoes an extensive application process. I had to submit previous annual fitness reports, a list of duties and achievements since joining the navy, letters of recommendation from my commanding officer and the senior hospital administrator written in navyspeak (an "excellent job" means mediocre, but an "outstanding job" means top dog), proof of continuing education, copies of my orders, and so on.

The augmentation board met once a year. Being passed over

once is expected, but after the second time, the résumé needs fattening up. This process was under way well before I began angling for promotion. I became a poster child for the navy party line, wearing my uniform perfectly and proudly, becoming politically savvy in my interactions with senior officers and their spouses, going to conventions in uniform, and attending gatherings of navy and other military psychologists. I presented papers, participated on panels, and got medals.

Despite all my efforts, I wasn't augmented.

I am a resilient person with perhaps an overabundance of perseverance. With each "no" that I received, I just tried harder or attempted to find another way to achieve the goal. Because I seemed to believe that I had a direct and irrefutable pipeline to God, it never occurred to me that my staying in the navy might not be God's plan for me.

I had become like the logger who kept chopping away on the same piece of wood that was simply not going to split open because it was being struck in the wrong place. It didn't matter how much I beat my head against the wall or banged on the door, if it wasn't God's will, it wasn't going to happen.

At the same time, I wasn't doing anything to displease God. I wasn't breaking any commandments. I wasn't harming anyone else. I wasn't really even hurting myself. While I was busy trying to achieve my own will by getting augmented or promoted, I got a tremendous amount of professional and administrative experience, which paid off later.

As I reflect back on that period of my life, I now realize that the wood may have actually been split perfectly. I just misunderstood the use that it was to be put to. It seems that my single-minded pursuit of self-will, trying to achieve the results that I wanted, helped prepare me for other plans that God had for me. Maybe that was the point, the preparation for what was to come after the navy, not the navy career itself. Maybe stubbornness and perseverance had paid off after all.

Through the failed experience with gaining augmentation, I learned some hard but important lessons: Don't outline for God.

God makes straight crooked paths. And, of course, Father (God) always knows best.

Here are some guidelines for discerning God's will:

1. Ask each day for knowledge of God's will and the power to carry it out.
2. Assume that you are doing God's will if you have asked to do so and if your actions don't break any of His commandments or in any way harm you or others.
3. Review your considered or chosen course of action with someone who understands your desire to live life according to God's plan. Take the feedback you get seriously, since it is probably God speaking to you through this person.
4. Know that if you are sure that some plan or goal is God's will, but the doors keep closing no matter how hard you try to make it happen, it probably isn't His plan.
5. If you have prayed, consulted with a spiritual guide, and the doors open with ease, then congratulations! You can be assured, to the greatest extent possible for a mere human, that you are functioning within God's will for you.
6. Are you doing something just to please someone else, to get approval? Are you choosing an action to avoid having feelings or because it feels good, rather than because it is good? Are you taking the easy way out to escape conflict or to achieve peace at any price? If you can answer "yes" to any of these questions, you are likely to be acting out of self-will.
7. Is your stomach churning and adrenaline pumping? Are you discounting the still small voice within (your intuition or the Spirit) and telling yourself that your feelings are wrong? Guess what? You are likely to be acting or making decisions out of self-will.
8. When you feel truly at peace in what you are planning or doing and no major obstacles are thrown in your way, you are likely to be living in God's will.
9. When you are fully awake and aware, living with God in the present moment, then you are in God's will.

Now you have come to know God, you have learned to trust Him, and He's become your best friend. You love God and enjoy spending time with Him. You've gotten the hang of trying to do God's will and follow His lead, and you have come to believe that He really does know what will work for you and what won't. But God isn't satisfied with this. He wants more, and He invites you into an ever deeper, more intimate relationship. God wants you to make a life commitment, and He invites you to surrender.

Chapter 7

Surrendering to God's Will

Surrender has never come easily to me. I have always had a strong personality. The main problem with this was that my mom and big sister, older by five and a half years, also had this trait in great abundance. I used to describe the women in my family as Mama Tank, Big Sister Tank, and Baby Tank. The baby was me, and there was no way I could go up against them.

I especially couldn't stand up to my mother. She seemed too powerful for me to risk confronting. My only choice was to buckle under and do whatever she wanted. The price of that surrender was that I had to deny myself totally by suppressing my feelings and opinions, always pretending that I agreed with her—to the point where I actually thought that I did. I avoided making any decisions without her approval, and I failed to develop likes and dislikes of my own.

I heard my mom loud and clear with her myriad directions, most of which I didn't want to follow. I thought her expectations were ridiculous, and I didn't believe I could measure up to them anyway. Besides, they didn't seem to have anything to do with me. Instead, they had to do with whether people would like me if I dressed a certain way (never anything shocking, just not her taste), whether anyone would marry me if I were overweight, what her friends would think if I didn't show up at an event where I didn't know, or wished I didn't know, anyone.

I wished I could tune out by withdrawing, watching TV, or saying "yes" when I clearly meant "no," then go and do whatever I wanted. But these talents for avoiding Mama Tank were the survival skills employed by my dad and my brother Ricky (now affectionately known as Bear). I had no ability to effectively space out.

Here is an example of the dialogue that went on regularly between my mother and brother.

> Mom (on her way out on a Saturday night): "Don't forget to do your Sunday school homework before you go to bed."
>
> Ricky (mumbling): "Uh-huh."
>
> Mom (apparently thinking he hadn't heard her): "I said, 'Don't forget to do your Sunday school homework before you go to sleep tonight.'"
>
> (Ricky, ignoring her, says nothing.)
>
> Mom (getting exasperated): "Did you hear me?"
>
> Ricky (tuning her out): "Mm-hmm."
>
> Mom (now taking a senseless risk): "What did I say?"
>
> Ricky (Oops! Busted! And very annoyed): "Take a shower and brush my teeth."

I got away from home as soon as I could and began to live a life of quiet, sometimes not so quiet, rebellion. Since I hadn't gotten married and had no prospects (part of the rebellion?), I left for college at the University of Wisconsin, a comfortable nine hundred miles away from home. I went to an endless string of fraternity parties, worked on the independent college newspaper, fervently cheered for the Badgers football team (who went to the Rose Bowl that year but lost), and always did just enough to get by.

I had boyfriends, but never anyone my mother would approve of. There was Joe, the heroin addict hairdresser, and Frank, the alcoholic taxi driver who had just been released from the state hospital. You get the idea.

Between diets, I overate. I was often out of control in my behavior. I was always overeating, overdrinking, ignoring my schoolwork so I had to take incompletes, chasing a guy, or breaking up. Then, in the next breath, I might stop everything and become a workaholic to catch up. Everything was in excess, but never all at once. That way, no one could accurately figure out just what my problem was.

Eventually, it became apparent to me (probably ages after everyone else in my life had noticed) that I was making a mess out of my life. Applying all my considerable—but in this instance useless—intelligence to figure a way out of my problems had failed to get me out of the deep hole I had dug for myself. It appeared that I would have to give up any illusion I had of power and control over anything.

It was clear that I would have to ask for help. But the idea of giving up and accepting direction from any higher power was a scary proposition, since my only experience had been submitting to my mother. We know how that went.

For me, surrendering had meant obliterating myself, my ideas and opinions, my beliefs, even my taste in clothing, men, music, or anything else that mattered to me. The word "surrender" smacked of a need for my mom's approval—a need so desperate that I had often put aside my own better judgment and self-esteem to win it. Rebellion, above all, helped me to maintain the illusion of independence. *I'm doing this on my own terms in my own way.*

Many people think of surrender as giving up or giving in, turning over the reins to someone or something else. It may be a voluntary choice, but often it is forced. It always involves a power struggle, and for good or for evil, one side always wins. Depending upon the circumstance and individual involved, it can result in turmoil or peace.

The type of surrender that I'm talking about is central to all spiritual and religious paths. Surrender, in this context, involves a value choice to completely give up your own will in favor of the will of a divine power. In other words, it means letting go and letting God determine your thoughts, words, actions, and attitudes.

Surrender is essential to Judaism (bow to one God), Christianity ("He who loses his life will gain it"), Islam (the word itself means submission as the path to peace), and Buddhism (surrender the attachments that cause suffering). There is no spiritual path that excludes the necessity of giving up power to some higher authority.

Surrender to win! This is the paradoxical outcome of letting go of your self, or ego, to make way for God. It is both giving up and gaining. Your life stance becomes openhanded, palms raised up to receive while God continuously gives. Such yielding sets in motion the probability of conversion from negative to positive behavior, thought, and feeling. When you have surrendered to God, you will be a healthier, more balanced, and more peaceful person.

The problem is that surrender, though positive and healthy in its highest spiritual form, is viewed as giving up, as a weakness, from the perspective of our culture. It is associated with subjugation and submission, a loss of control and power to questionable or even cruel authority. It implies being at the mercy of an authority who can decide to give or take away everything—freedom, pleasure, interests, activities, behaviors. It is experienced as a loss of rights and dignity, becoming a prisoner to another's will. It feels like an essential loss of self.

Surrendering control often leaves us with an overwhelming sense of powerlessness. Throughout our lives, we fight against the knowledge that we are essentially powerless. Yet, a baby's denial of dependency is necessary for survival.

An infant believes that she is powerful because every time she cries, babbles, smiles, or grunts, something happens. A big person will come along and feed her, change her, pick her up, pat her, smile, make faces at her, or even yell at her.

It is not until a child reaches the terrible twos that he begins to learn that he is just a midget in a land of giants. Now he begins to explore his world and hopefully learns that the adults in his life are trustworthy and will protect him from harm.

When an infant or child is seriously neglected, she will often end up in the hospital, refusing food and comfort, turning her head to the wall and dying. I believe this comes from being forced to experience her powerlessness before she is ready, never having had the chance to learn to trust.

Eventually, we learn to deal with frightening or overwhelming life circumstances by trying to control feelings of anxiety and uncertainty. The false belief that we have power over people and circumstances outside ourselves leads us to demand, like a baby, to have every wish fulfilled right now. When our demands aren't met immediately, we feel rejected and unloved.

Next, we put on the armor of defiance. Reality is denied, and we continue with behaviors and attitudes that are bound to cause trouble. Rebellion gives the false feeling of inner strength and self-confidence. *Nothing can happen to me!*

What are we denying? Any truth that seems too painful to face.

• • •

Maybe my family wasn't like the Cleavers, after all. Perhaps my parents weren't so happy. Could be that they were fighting about Dad's drinking. Does that mean he wasn't a social drinker? Was my mom actually mean to me? All that loving might have been overprotectiveness, keeping me from developing self-confidence.

• • •

I always thought I had a great marriage, but in truth, I feel neglected by him. He's always gone, working so that he can provide for us. I'm really lonely.

• • •

Since we had the baby, I feel like I don't count anymore. I guess she's a great mom, but I feel like yelling, "Look at me, won't you?"

• • •

I was sure I had a great future with this company. But they seem to recognize others and not appreciate me. I thought loyalty and hard work would pay off.

• • •

I was so proud of my kids. But despite all my teaching, they keep doing things that will cause them hurt and harm. And when they're gone, who will watch over them—and who will I be?

• • •

I never expected to have to go through all these painful things: sickness, loss, disappointment, death of my child, abuse by my parent, loss of my innocence. Where was God then? I feel like a total victim. Life isn't fair. Where was God when I needed Him? Why did God allow these things to happen? I feel empty and betrayed, and my life seems meaningless. My drinking isn't working anymore. I'm still depressed, but I don't want to stop. I need something to fix me.

. . .

I had been in the navy only six weeks when I was sent to the Alcohol Rehabilitation Service for a two-week course to learn how to recognize and treat or refer alcoholics and compulsive overeaters. I was put in a group with the alcoholics and overeaters and told to use the group as my own. I told the group that I was a potential alcoholic and overeater, but I was controlling these behaviors "very successfully, thank you very much!"

I was far away from home with no friends or family. This was my first job since earning my doctorate in psychology. I needed people to like me, and I wanted to be successful. I had no one to turn to, advise me, comfort me, or cover up for me.

My group counselor during this visiting doctors program was Mike, a tall, silver-haired paraprofessional, a recovering alcoholic who appeared to me to be full of himself because he had treated a president's wife, a senator, an astronaut, and a few admirals. I couldn't stand him because he shredded his patients with the truth. Or so it seemed to arrogant, defiant me!

Mike had the nerve to tell me, "I would never refer anyone to you for treatment. You are way too screwed up to be able to help anyone else."

I went to the psychiatrist who directed the program to complain about Mike. Captain Pursch offered to transfer me to another group, but I sullenly and self-righteously told him that I wouldn't think of undermining Mike's authority with his patients. I would stay. The fact of the matter was that I knew, at some level, that Mike was the first person to tell me the truth about myself. It was terrifying, but necessary, to discover.

Know the truth and the truth will set you free, but first it will make you miserable!

I was backed against the wall. I had held on to old behaviors and beliefs about myself, others, and the world long past the point of usefulness. I had to surrender to the truth about myself.

I have heard that the Chinese character for crisis is the same as the one for opportunity. This is just what this state of affairs proved to be for me—a crisis not only causing me to panic and pay attention but also providing me with an opportunity to start again in a new way. It was obvious that running my life based on my own decisions and my own will had not been a great success. So I felt that the only real chance I had of changing the outcomes in my life required willingness to give up self-will in favor of God's will.

As it turned out, the fact that I'd made a decision to give up and let God be in charge didn't mean that I found it easy to do so. Continuing to live the way I had up until now was out of the question. It felt like now or never. I had to surrender.

What? Surrender? You've got to be kidding! Who in their right mind wants to surrender?

Many women fight surrender because they associate this word with experiences of being controlled, dominated, ordered, commanded, and abused. A friend of mine who grew up in a violent home said that surrender meant giving up part of herself, her rights as a child and later as a woman. When life got too painful for her, even after being out of that abusive home for years, giving herself up to God (another man, in her view) was overwhelmingly difficult and seemed to involve great risk.

Men, on the other hand, hate the idea of surrender because it seems weak and unmanly. It means giving up. History is full of men who refused to surrender even when continuing on their course of action meant certain death, destruction, or failure. Consider Pharaoh of ancient biblical infamy, the Israelites wandering in the desert, Napoleon's frozen soldiers fighting a war on two fronts, and the United States carrying on too long in Vietnam.

I used to work with Vietnam veterans. Now there's a group of people, both men and women, who had strong reason to dislike the word "surrender." They fought long and hard, lost their youth and innocence, lost faith in the purpose for the struggle, and felt betrayed by their government, military leadership, and fellow Americans. If America surrendered, then what was it all for? But the truth of the matter was that though they may not have liked the terms of the surrender, they were clearly better off to be at peace than at war.

Though the war was over in Vietnam in the minds of the American people and in the attitudes of the government, many Vietnam war vets weren't able to personally surrender. These brave men and women were still at war within. Nightmares, flashbacks, checking perimeters for an exit in case danger appeared, startle reactions to fireworks on the Fourth of July, difficulty with intimacy—all made an adjustment to life after the external conflict ended very difficult. To achieve any degree of internal peace required acceptance of the reality of their struggle, willingness to talk about their experiences, and trust that their emotions wouldn't ultimately do them in. To move on required another surrender, this time to hope and faith that God could and would heal them.

During the late 1990s, I worked for an innovative, respected, and successful company providing outpatient treatment for chemical dependency. When the founder of the company, a visionary and a great man, died, he was replaced by Mark, a businessman whose previous accomplishment was turning a small family-owned hamburger diner into a successful restaurant chain. The idea was that he would repeat his previous performance by taking this small group of three or four clinics and growing them into a similarly successful chain of treatment centers. He would add some residential and inpatient treatment, thereby covering all levels of care. Then he would make it into a franchise operation.

By the time Mark was adding the seventh outpatient clinic and trying to contract with a local hospital, the little company began to topple. There were so many costs accrued by administrative priorities that the clinics stopped making money.

At that time, I was the director of clinical operations. Contracts weren't working out. Projects that got started kept falling through.

It seemed to me that our determined and inappropriately fearless leader might be knocking his head repeatedly against an inflexible wall. I thought he would do well to give up and go back to the basics that had originally brought success.

The company's treatment program was spiritually based, with a foundation in the Twelve Step program of Alcoholics Anonymous. Everyone, staff and patients alike, was constantly talking about God or a Higher Power. But Mark didn't understand alcoholism or chemical dependency, and I don't think he understood the deeply spiritual nature of the program. So the idea that perhaps it wasn't God's will to continue with his proposed course of action didn't occur to him. Mark was determined to make it happen the way he thought it should. In the end, his self-will pushed the company to the brink of failure. It had to be sold, and four of the seven clinics were closed. Eventually, they all went out of business.

And so it is with presidents and premiers and queens and CEOs and husbands and wives and gang leaders and junkies and rich and poor.

When defiance and grandiosity finally push an individual to a point where they can no longer effectively function, an act of surrender can occur. When this happened to me, I became receptive to new information. I could listen and learn without fighting back. I was wide open to seeing myself as I really am and the world as it really is.

Letting go connected me to my true self, shedding light on my dark and hidden places and allowing me to give up the lies, games, and masks I'd used to protect my true self from discovery. I began the difficult and painful process of dying to my false self, to my previous ways of being, which I had always used to preserve the illusion of control over my life. Surrender forced me to become vulnerable before God, who knew and loved me before I knew or loved myself.

Emma is my friend and colleague, a fellow spiritual director. While we were still students in our spiritual direction training program, I asked for her take on the act of surrender. Her mother's cancer, her brother's death, and her children's worry that the world, as we know it, is not a place where they would want to raise a new generation prompted her to turn to God, deepen her faith, and trust in the act of surrender.

"For me," Emma observed, "surrender is like flying on a trapeze. I have to let go of the bar and trust in the timing of the Spirit moving within me and in the outstretched arms of my God who will grasp me." She went on to say, "It is only in these 'letting go's' in life that God can teach us to fly." Emma describes having a sense of God holding her and carrying her through whatever is put in front of her as soon as she lets go.

What are the fruits of surrender that are so sweet that I arrived at a point where I valued, even desired, surrender?

- I have found that when I give up and give over to God, I am better able to accept reality as it is. I no longer strive to make over people and circumstances into my view of how they should or ought to be.
- I can discern the truth and make changes, with God's help, in my own attitudes and reactions.
- When I am in an ongoing state of surrender, my capacity to accept myself and others as we really are persists, and I am better able to live and function comfortably, without anger or fear.
- I can accept responsibility and have the freedom to make life better for myself and for those around me.
- I can usually tell how deeply I have accepted reality by how relaxed I am. I'm not fighting anyone or anything.
- I'm more positive, more creative, and more spontaneous.
- I'm more in touch with my inner voice, and I experience deeper peace and serenity.
- In a state of sweet surrender, I can experience every feeling and event fully. Finding meaning in all things, I go before God in prayer as I truly am—happy, sad, broken, angry, petty, lost, at peace—not as I think I ought to be. There are no more masks; there's just me, and that's okay.

Before I learned to entrust the positive power of surrender to a powerful and loving God, I lived out of ego needs. I was always fighting some battle or another, trying to attain power or prestige or fame or dominance or approval or recognition or love or sanity or whatever else I might have thought I was lacking or had to have or hold on to. It escaped me that the only ambition that would bring peace and happiness was to live life surrendered to God's loving care.

Surrender comes slowly, often paced over a lifetime. I gave up only a little of myself at first. At each step of the way, whenever a new problem came up, I first tried to ignore it, then tried to control it. Each time, I've had to confront my powerlessness and the mess I make when I try to handle it on my own. I rarely deal with my problems by immediately surrendering to God, though I'm definitely getting better at turning to God more quickly. I'm continuously amazed at how awesome God's solutions are when I simply surrender, asking for His will, not mine, to be done.

If You Pray for Potatoes, You'd Better Be Prepared to Pick Up the Hoe

God wants to answer our prayers. I think He wants to say "Yes!" when I tell Him what's on my mind and what it is that I want. The thing is that often the meaning I attach to a request and God's interpretation of it can be two very different things. After all, my vision of what is possible and good is severely limited compared with God's.

Alice was my dear friend. She was quite a bit older than me, and I looked up to her for her wisdom and her apparent contentment with her life despite many trials she had endured. I liked her because she was somewhat eccentric, an eighty-year-old imp with flaming red hair, beatnik style skirts and shawls, a majestic manner of speaking, and boundless energy.

She could summarize a situation with a few well-chosen words. She was direct, wasting no time getting to the point. If she offered advice, she wrapped it in a parable about her own experience. If you took her advice, that was fine. And if you didn't, she loved you anyway.

Alice had a wonderful marriage to a spiritually gifted former priest. It was a marriage based on their mutual love of God and desire to do His will, respect for one another, shared interests, and willingness to allow differing points of view.

Seven years after I began to fall in love with God, I asked Alice how she and Ed came to be together. She said that it was clearly God's answer to her prayer. For several years, she had prayed for God to send someone to love her. No one came. One day, she decided to change her prayer. Instead, she asked God to send someone for her to love.

I thought that was really cool. I sat down that very night and told God that I was ready and willing to have someone in my life to love.

He answered my prayer all right. While I was waiting for a tall, dark, handsome, rich, and spiritual guy on whom to pour out my love, God had a different version of an answer to my prayer. A mere six months later, I was pregnant, and the wonderful guy on whom I was going to pour out all my love was nowhere to be found. Within a year, I had an amazing little baby girl.

Four months after my daughter, Shaina, was born, my father came to live with us. He was still grief-stricken over my mother's death two years earlier, and he was in the early stages of dementia.

My dad lived with his granddaughter and me for seven years. He felt wanted, needed, and loved, especially by Shaina, who was the apple of his eye. He gave us both tender love and affection. But as she grew older, he grew younger until they switched places. When my daughter was four years old, they went for a walk. When they arrived home, he was carrying my tearful daughter.

"What's wrong?" I asked her as I took her into my arms.

"We got lost," she said sniffling. Then she added indignantly, "And Pop-Pop wouldn't listen to me when I tried to tell him the right way to go."

My father had indeed become my younger child.

For the first time in my life, I had two people who needed me. I learned to put their needs in front of my own. I took my dad to the doctor and made sure he got meals appropriate for his medical needs. I arranged day care, not just for one, but for both.

When Shaina was seven, I found a caregiver named Anna who

came to work in my home. While I was working, Anna became the "taxi" driver to get my daughter to gymnastics and my dad to appointments. Anna prepared their meals and watched out for their safety.

One night, I arrived home from work at 10:30 p.m. after seeing several evening patients. As I walked in the door, Anna came running out, yelling, "I've had it. It's too much. I've cooked at a country club for hundreds of people at a time. I thought cooking for one seven-year-old girl and one seventy-seven-year-old man would be simple. But it's impossible to please these two. I quit!"

By the next morning, I had to come up with a viable solution so that I could go to work. It was important to try to stay at least somewhat calm while I did what I had to do to take care of these two individuals I loved so dearly.

Together, they smoothed away many of my rough edges. Slowly, as a result of loving and caring for them, I became softer, gentler, more patient and tolerant, and more the person God made me to be.

God's plan for me was better than mine was. God does answer prayer. So be careful what you pray for. When you pray for potatoes, you'd better be prepared to pick up the hoe!

Leading a Spiritual Life Requires a Willingness to Be Surprised by God

When I realized that a career in the navy was not in the books for me, I was devastated. When you get passed over for promotion in the navy, no one tells you why. The proceedings of the promotion board are kept secret. It's not public information who's on the board. It would be impossible to say whether it was God's will that I get out of the navy or whether I had made someone who happened to be on the current promotion committee angry with me.

When I was the clinical director of the Alcohol Rehabilitation Service, I was often put in the position of confronting officers who were senior to me regarding their apparent alcoholism. If an officer agreed, decided to enter treatment, and stayed sober, he would always be grateful for my intervention. If an officer, after being confronted, didn't enter treatment—well, you can imagine how that person might have felt toward me.

At one point, I was ordered to do an investigation of an accident caused by a former psychiatric inpatient. When I began to question the psych techs, nurses, and others in his department, the chief of psychiatry became extremely unhappy with me. He told me to stay off the psychiatric ward and away from his staff. If I didn't, he assured me, he would use his political connections to block any chance I had of promotion.

I don't know exactly why I didn't get promoted. It's not really important to me anymore. God knows how to make straight crooked paths. Everyone has free will, complete liberty to think, make choices, and act as they see fit, given their circumstances. Often however, we're in the path of other people's bad behavior and self-centered attitudes. Though God may not prevent actions or events that are distressful, painful, or disturbing from happening, He is there to help us through, strongly and steadily, to comfort us, and to guide us on our path as we courageously move on.

With only three or four months left before I was discharged into civilian life, I had to figure out what to do next. I wanted to be an administrator or director of a residential or inpatient chemical dependency treatment program. I began interviewing for some exciting positions in Chicago, Texas, and Colorado.

Then I discovered that I was pregnant. I decided it wasn't a good idea just then to leave my friends and support system to move to another state a thousand miles away. Another "no" from God?

I began interviewing for jobs closer to home, perhaps a little less exciting, but acceptable. Each time I thought I was really close to an offer for a position, I would inform the potential employer that I was pregnant and would have to be out on maternity leave in a few months' time.

Seemingly sure bets, those jobs never materialized. Finally, I was offered a position as a counselor for an up-and-coming intensive outpatient treatment company. My hours were to be 2 p.m. to 10 p.m. I was not a happy camper. I had wanted to be an administrator, not a counselor. I knew nothing about outpatient treatment, and I wasn't thrilled to work until 10 at night.

How was I to know that I would eventually be promoted to

management within this company and would help it grow from two to seven clinics? How was I to know that intensive outpatient treatment was the wave of the future, and I was to be one of the first to help develop it as a viable method of treatment? How was I to know that, in its earliest days, I would become familiar with and known to managed care personnel, thus helping me several years later when I wanted to start a private practice? How was I to know that working afternoons and evenings would allow me to spend time with my infant daughter during the most awake and lively hours of her day?

I had to admit that although I had nothing in my life that I'd ever wanted, what I had was better than anything I'd ever dreamed of. This has happened many times in my life. So when God closes a door in your life, hang on and hang in. And remember, living a spiritual life requires a willingness to be surprised by God.

Surrender: Is It a Question of How or Whether?

The first difficulty with surrendering is making the decision to surrender. Without willingness, surrender is a nonstarter.

It isn't unusual to cling to old ways of doing things even when they're obviously not working or causing deep unhappiness.

• • •

I'm overweight and my self-esteem is in the toilet. My health is in jeopardy. I can't get down on the floor and play with my kids. But I love to eat. Food is my friend.

• • •

I love him. I know he doesn't treat me well. He loses his temper and belittles me, but I know he doesn't mean it.

• • •

I'm about to lose my job because I can't ever seem to get there on time. I have to get the kids off to school, and they refuse to get out of bed. Why won't my boss be more understanding? After all, I'm a really good worker.

• • •

My daughter can't seem to hold a job. I think it's because she drinks too much. She's twenty-six, and she's still living with me. She doesn't pay rent, she comes home in the middle of the night, and she never cleans up after herself. My friends all tell me to kick her out, but where would she go? I'm afraid she'd end up on the street, or worse.

. . .

We hang on to our own way of doing and seeing things until we run ourselves into the ground. If you're anything like me, you probably won't be willing to change until the consequences of your behavior or character traits become dire. Then you can no longer lie to yourself about how serious the situation is.

Often, before any significant change can take place, the support and protection provided in the past by family, friends, bosses, and co-workers must be removed. People, previously part of the safety net, withdraw in disgust or exhaustion from their futile attempts at helping.

When we can no longer drag up enough energy to be angry or defiant, when we are unhappy or frustrated enough or finally become sick and tired of being sick and tired, we become willing and open to make the decision to let go. It's time to stop the struggle, and we become teachable.

At every moment, we have a choice—be open or closed, hold on or let go, harden our hearts or soften them. We are never forced to let go, although sometimes it may feel that way. No one has to stop overeating, overspending, gambling, or drinking. No one has to be kind to an obnoxious neighbor or loving to out-of-control children. No one has to be forgiving of the person who has caused hurt and anguish. No one has to listen to God or try to discern or do His will.

Grumbling every step of the way, I might avoid offering my will to God. But then I hear in my mind the voice of my beloved and much missed surrogate mom, who passed away several years ago.

Ruthie would have said to me, "Judith, you don't have to want to, you just have to do it."

So I give in and turn my will over to God. And just like that, what seems like giving in and giving up turns into blessings, self-esteem, and peace.

Is it always right to let go? Aren't there times when persistence is appropriate? Of course there are. Letting go and persistence are not necessarily opposed to one another if the desired outcome is ultimately doing it God's way. Surrendering to God doesn't mean sitting by the road waiting for good results of my prayer to happen.

There is the story of the man who had an absolutely beautiful garden. His friend was visiting him and commented, "My, what a beautiful garden God has given you."

The man answered, "Yeah? Well, you should have seen it when God had it alone!"

One of Jesus' parables is about a man who wakes up his neighbor in order to borrow some food so he could be hospitable to an unexpected guest. The neighbor wants nothing to do with it. He wants to be left alone to sleep. The man persists until the neighbor gives in, not because it was the right thing to do, but because he was worn down by the man's repeated asking. God responds to our persistence, not necessarily by giving us exactly what we ask for, but by filling us with His spirit and love so that we can better know His will and desires for us.

Persistence is always appropriate if you are having trouble doing or not doing something you know is God's will. Then the thing to do is to continually pray for willingness to make the decision and take the ongoing action to accomplish your goal. Once you get started on the right path, every day, every hour, or every minute, pray for the strength to "keep on keeping on."

What often happens is that people give in temporarily to the need to change. They can see that they're in a world of trouble, and they take action. But underneath the surface compliance lurks the unconscious thought, "I'll do this for now, but as soon as things clear up . . ." This is merely conditional surrender with no real acceptance of the need to change. The struggle is therefore bound to recur. The effects of the initial letting go slowly wear off, and the original state of mind and behavior return.

I'm always struggling with overeating and losing weight. I'll get really fed up with myself, and start to eat right. I feel great. My weight begins to stabilize; my energy level improves; I feel good about myself. *This time it will be different. Yes, I know it's different. I have it wired. I've learned my lesson. I've given up. Well, maybe I could have just a small piece of that birthday cake.* And I'm off and running again.

Help me, God. Forgive me, God. Why does this keep happening, God? Why won't I truly give up? I'm back to feeling awful and praying for willingness.

When surrender occurs, it's like getting a new pair of glasses. There is an infusion of hope and faith. The problem that had been an implacable thorn in the side is seen with a completely new perspective.

Unfortunately, surrender never fixes itself in the personality. It requires daily action of letting go and living life this new way.

Once you've decided to give your life to God, you'll be ready to apply this new attitude or approach to life. If you're new to the business of surrender, you're probably feeling scared or overwhelmed. You don't know where to start or how. Here are some suggestions:

1. First of all, identify the thing you want to give up. Remind yourself that there is a God, and it isn't you. Let God be the pilot while you assist Him as the copilot.

2. If you're too scared to let go, ask God for willingness. Tell Him, "I really don't want to give up _____. So, if it's all the same to You, let me out of this challenge. But if You insist, then let Your will, not mine, be done."

3. Next ask God for help and guidance. "God (or use your name for your Higher Power), I offer myself to you. Please take away (name the problem)." Some examples of attitudes to be given up are arrogance, always expecting to be a victim, self-righteousness, low self-esteem. Thoughts might include obsessive worry about the bills, the kids,

the girlfriend's disapproval, the boss's failure to praise you. Behaviors could be overdrinking, overspending, chronic lateness, being too loud or argumentative, never standing up for yourself, gossiping, or lying.

4. Start with smaller problems or less threatening areas of your life. This will help you build some trust in the process and in God. It's a little like getting your big toe wet before diving into the pool's cold water.

5. If the problem you are confronting is one that is ruining your health, marriage, family, or job, you may have to take the plunge right away. If this is the case, take it easy. Don't think of doing or not doing this one seemingly huge and insurmountable thing for a lifetime but only for this moment, this hour, this day.

6. Sit before God, offering yourself in all your brokenness. Pray and meditate. Briefly notice and reflect on how you hold on to the old behavior or idea. Acknowledge it, and let it go.

7. Imagine putting the problem into a helium balloon and letting it go, floating upward to God. Imagine placing the person, situation, or anguish on a dumbwaiter, pressing the button, and sending it up to God. Imagine the distressing thought resting on a puffy white cloud; then watch as the cloud moves across the sky away from you.

8. Make a symbolic gesture of surrender or purification. Write out the issue on a piece of paper. Make it a letter to God. Or, if you're angry, write a letter, not for sending, to the person you're mad at. Get it all out on paper. Take a box, make a slit in its lid, and label it your God Box. Drop the writing in the box. Or get a coffee can for your paper, and label it your God Can because God can. Or put it in your Bible or another spiritual book. Or burn it.

9. I have a painting of Jesus in prayer hanging in my bedroom. I cut a slit in the framing paper on the back of it, and when I have a really big, hard, or painful thing to let go of, I write to God and put the letter there. That way, I can't take it out or take it back.

10. If you're unable to sleep because you're worrying about many things, write out a list of those things. At the bottom of the list, tell God that you really need your rest, and you know He is staying up all night anyway. Ask God to take care of these things while you sleep.

11. When all else fails to distract you from the problem at hand, be of service or help someone else.

Each surrender to God will prepare you and give you courage for the next round of letting go. As you change and grow, you'll always find new behaviors, attitudes, or thoughts that need to be relinquished. There will be repeated opportunities to shed old skin as new life challenges appear.

As you gain experience, you'll notice that anything you do to hold on to a problem or avoid letting go only causes greater pain. When the hurt becomes intolerable, you just want it to go away. Then you'll remember that "letting go and letting God" brings peace. The determination to hang on will be replaced with an overwhelming desire for the fruits of letting go. You have learned the true meaning of surrender to win.

Lest you think that the spiritual path and relationship with God is characterized by a straight line to the stars, unwavering commitment, fairy tale romance, and happiness, I should probably warn you that this is rarely the case. As in any relationship that matures over a lifetime, there are always cycles that parallel the seasons—the shedding of old habits or immaturities, the lying fallow, and then the emergence of new blossoms and ripe fruit of shared life experience. Life tends to teach, not always gracefully, the meaning of "for better or for worse, for richer or for poorer, in sickness and in health from this day forward." We hope for "better," "richer," and "health," but that's not always what we get. Life partners who face difficulties together and continue to love one another exactly as they are gain the rich fruits of a lifelong intimate relationship.

God wants no less from us in our relationship with Him. God wants us to love Him for Himself. And all spiritual seekers, mystics, or theologians, clergy or commoner, experience darkness and light, joy and sorrow in leading a spiritual life and pursuing a life-long committed relationship with God. All of us, at some time in our spiritual journey, have to learn how to cope when we face disappointment, doubt, or difficulty in our relationship with God.

At this stage in my path, I had begun to develop the skills necessary to be a "spiritual warrior" when darkness comes.

Chapter 8

Taking It Back,
or You Can't Be Serious, God

I must have been nuts. How had I deluded myself so thoroughly? I really, truly thought I could do this surrender thing. I had genuinely meant it when I said, "Your will, not mine, be done."

Apparently, I fell far short of my own expectations. Somehow, I had come to believe that since I was such a good girl, living such a clean, upright, hardworking, and spiritual life, God would give me whatever I wanted. And I also must have believed that whatever I desired would coincide with God's plan. At any rate, my wishes, hopes, and dreams weren't bad. There wasn't anything intrinsically wrong or evil about them. So what would be the big deal for God to grant them? It wouldn't be any skin off of His glorious nose to make my plans and dreams come true, would it?

Doesn't scripture say, "Ask and you shall receive"? Doesn't it say that if we pray believing, we can move mountains? Maybe that's what it literally meant—move mountains, not any of the simpler things that could actually occur.

There I was, praying to give myself to God absolutely. "Take all of me, Lord. Let me give of myself to You and not count the cost."

What did I get for all my praying, going to church, and attempts to be good? I'll tell you what I didn't get. I didn't get promoted. I didn't get to Japan. I didn't get that tall, dark, handsome, and spiritual knight in shining armor. I didn't get the administrative position in a residential treatment center. I didn't get my way.

If I had known this is how God would be when I started out, would I have even started? Another disappointment. Another failed relationship. Another heartbreak.

I was hurt, angry, and disappointed. I was lost, and I had no bearings. God had been my true north. Now, it seemed that everything I thought I knew about Him was being challenged.

Sometimes We Are Struck with a Rebellion of Spirit So Sickening That We Can't Even Pray

In an instant, I went from an extreme pray-er to someone who couldn't stand the thought of talking to God under any circumstances. I clearly remember that moment. It was like being struck by a bolt of lightning or shaken to the core by an earthquake.

Five years into my spiritual journey, I became obsessed with being perfect for God. I decided to seek spiritual direction. This is an undertaking that, on the surface, is somewhat similar to counseling, yet it is really quite different. Here, the primary focus is on my relationship with God, trying to understand what God is calling me to do or to understand in my life. It is an attempt to discover through prayer what is moving me closer to God and what might be drawing me away from Him.

My spiritual director was a generous and loving woman named Martha. I visited her home on a weekly basis, and she helped me to feel comfortable and safe during my visits. Sometimes her husband, Ruben, assisted Martha in directing me. They were both dedicated to their church and had worked together as a team for many years, leading Marriage Encounter weekends, providing individual spiritual direction, and directing people like me in the Spiritual Exercises of Saint Ignatius.

I viewed Martha and Ruben as soul friends who were trained to assist me in deepening my prayer life. They would teach me to take my feelings and experiences to God in prayer and listen for his response or reaction.

I was referred to Martha for the specific purpose of undertaking the Spiritual Exercises, an intense, structured program of prayer that is usually done on a thirty-day silent retreat. Since I couldn't leave my job and life for that period of time and since thirty days of silence seemed extremely intimidating, I chose to follow the method where each week of prayer carried out in everyday life is equivalent to one day of the silent retreat method. The process takes thirty weeks instead of thirty days.

Though Martha was enthusiastic about directing me, she expressed, somewhat ominously, that she always had some trepidation about starting the Spiritual Exercises with a new person. She told me that people's lives often changed radically during the process, and sometimes the changes were painful.

Perhaps I was called by God to do the exercises. On the other hand, it may have been more spiritual pride, attempting to be a prayer warrior when I was still pretty much a newcomer to a committed relationship with God. Either way, I proceeded to plunge in with naive enthusiasm.

During the next eight months or so, I experienced many losses. My mother died suddenly. I struggled with a great deal of guilt over the fact that I was not as upset about her loss as I believed I should be. I had not been close to her, but our relationship had improved over the years. Because my dad worked in the shoe industry, my parents had lived in Spain for thirteen years at the time of her death. I was used to her being far away, and I had found great comfort in my relationship with Ruthie, who had become a surrogate mother to me.

What was really painful for me was the knowledge that my dad's heart was breaking, and I was worried about how he would fare without my mom, his soul mate of more than forty-eight years. He was halfway around the world and alone.

Next, I was passed over for promotion, and my orders to Japan were canceled. I had been so sure that being in the navy and helping people in Japan and other parts of the world were my God-given mission. I had been preparing for promotion and transfer to Japan with nearly complete tunnel vision. Now, I felt adrift and without purpose.

I had become deeply immersed in the process of detaching from worldly things and being attached to and depending only on God. The world as I knew it, and as I expected it to be, was now turned upside down. I was angry, sad, and far from understanding what was happening to me. Now, my only anchor was God. That's what I had prayed for, right?

Shortly after I completed the exercises, I went to see my dad, who was visiting my family in Philadelphia. I had not seen my father since my mom's funeral. When I arrived home from my trip, Martha and Ruben met me at the airport. We went out for dinner, and I expressed my feelings of anger, hurt, confusion, and loss.

Ruben, probably in an attempt to comfort me, commented, "Our life on earth is just a dim reflection of the joy we will receive in heaven. All that you are doing and learning is just part of the journey to eternal life with God."

That was the moment I shut down.

Everything inside me screamed, *This is not okay. It has to be better than this. I have to be able to experience joy in this life. And if this is the best God can do for all the effort I've put in, forget it!*

I became angry with God and with myself. What made either of us think I was up to leading a prayerful life? What made me think I could abandon myself to Him totally, attaching myself to nothing but Him? What made God think I would be up to living a life that was not human, but superhuman or even saintly? I wanted to take it all back.

My prayer life became empty. I went through the motions, but I felt nothing. It became harder and harder to pray. I could not sit down and be quiet. I was not interested in listening. This is when I understood the meaning of the concept that "sometimes we are struck with a rebellion of spirit so sickening that we can't even pray."

In my head, I knew that I had to keep trying, but sometimes the best I could do was to say the Lord's Prayer while I was brushing my teeth, and I couldn't even keep track of that. Spiritual darkness was upon me.

Lord, I Believe; Help My Unbelief

I was going through the motions, more or less. It felt like God was in my head, not my heart. I had to learn that when love matures and the giddy, thrilling, overpowering, all-consuming sense of oneness passes, what appears is loving action. This is the fruit of true love—still being present, reliable, dependable, loyal, truthful, faithful, caring, and nurturing even when the thrill is gone. My love and commitment to my relationship with God were often demonstrated by these actions when I could no longer feel, or even trust, His presence.

If anyone asked, I could recount the many blessings in my life that were clearly gifts from God:

- By coming to know God more deeply through prayer, I had come to know myself better.
- I was able to acknowledge my assets and limitations, and I had come to accept myself as I am at any given moment in time.
- I had become financially responsible, paying my bills, avoiding debt, and not looking to others to bail me out.
- I no longer experienced the dire need for approval.
- I felt honored to be able to help those who came to me in need, and I was pleased that I did my work well.
- I often experienced myself as a channel for God, providing counsel to friends and patients alike. I was awed by that.
- I had become a softer, more loving person, and I was far less self-centered.
- I had come to deeply believe that God loves me, that I am His daughter and He is proud of me, that He made me and I am worthy in His eyes.

All of these changes were a direct result of having built a relationship with God through prayer—talking to Him and listening.

The external evidence of God's blessings in my life included the gift of my beautiful, talented, and awesome daughter, a rewarding job, wonderful friends, and freedom from a variety of self-defeating behaviors. I also had the opportunity to return the gift of my dad's love and protection by being able to care for him in his declining years.

Yet, despite all the evidence of God's good in my life, I was still afraid to trust Him. There were moments when I wondered if I had made up the whole God thing. Maybe God wasn't real. What if I was the highest power in my life, and I only had myself to depend upon?

With so many doubts and fears filling my head, with all the difficulty I was having with prayer and with all the distance and emptiness I felt in my relationship with God, I somehow carried on as if nothing had changed. I talked about God all the time—to my patients, to my friends, to anyone who came to me in need.

Though I sometimes felt like a hypocrite, I acted as if all was well between God and me because, in some deep way, I knew that all *was* well. I could sense God's power working through me and see the evidence of it in my life. This was both awesome and strange.

Throughout these times of spiritual darkness, this is the prayer that sustained me:

"Lord, I believe. Help my unbelief."

How to Survive the Darkness:
Being Blinded by the Light

Anyone who tries to live a life of prayer will eventually experience a time when the spiritual well has gone dry. This is a time of being in the wilderness, as Jesus was during the time that He was being tempted. The temptation for us is to give up prayer, feeling deserted by God. Jesus' trip into the desert wasn't initiated by the devil or some evil force, and neither is ours. Instead, it is God who leads us there, teaching us that prayer and the power derived through prayer cannot be controlled by the pray-er. It is the province of God to decide when His presence will be felt in gushes of warmth, love, sweetness, mystery, and mercy or when it won't be experienced at all.

It is exactly when we feel most abandoned and plunged into darkness that God is most present. God cautioned Moses not to look directly at Him or he would be blinded. Similarly, it is just when we feel most deeply that we have entered a smothering, inescapable dark night that God has come so close to us that we are blinded by His light.

But instead of being in awe of God's nearness, we tend to feel like a deer caught in the headlights—terrified. We're afraid that we're doing something wrong in our attempts to pray. Or we think we're being punished for some unacknowledged sin, or somehow we have displeased God.

In fact, the truth is quite the opposite. God is saying He is well pleased with our faithfulness. We have grown enough in our relationship with Him and, as a consequence, in our knowledge of ourselves that we are ready to be pruned. We are being stripped of whatever still remains of our old self, our ego, and our attachments so that we can be purified and renewed. Shedding the old self naturally involves pain and darkness. We want to hold on to what is familiar, old ways of thinking and communicating, even though these habits no longer work. They are, at least, comfortable. Letting go of ego and attachments means entering a new path in which everything seems strange and unfamiliar.

We are also being called to a new way of prayer in which we see that the living of life itself is a prayer. God is present in all people and all things, so the way we interact with others, our surroundings, and our environment becomes the basis of communication with Him.

God wants us to want Him for Himself, not just the *feeling* of Him. He desires our willingness to sit with Him in spite of the experience of emptiness, the overpowering sense of meaninglessness, the desire to run away, the inability to focus, and the total lack of satisfaction during our time with Him.

When we have fully committed ourselves to a spiritual path, we are likely, at some point, to experience the absence of consolation in prayer, a sense that we are doing something wrong and a seeming inability to pray in any way but formally. It might seem as if we are just going through the motions of a prayer life when, in truth, these are often signs that we're being led into the wilderness to become new again. The crowning evidence, to my way of thinking, of being in the darkness of God's light are the feelings of utter misery and unbearable loss and grief that come from missing Him, fearing that He is lost forever. The crowning glory is the call to pray beyond words, emotions, or human understanding. It's the ability to just be, as you find true peace in God's oneness with you.

Like me, you are probably wondering how to survive this cold and seemingly cruel winter. Here are some things I've learned along the way:

1. Look at the rest of your life. What is good? What changes have you undergone, what personal growth? How are you more loving, gentle, kind, generous? How do you acknowledge God in all people and all things? If you can answer these questions with the understanding that your thoughts, words, actions, and attitudes reflect a life that is God-centered, then you can be assured that the darkness is a gift, a calling from God.

2. Know that this is a normal part of prayer life. You are not doing something wrong to cause it.

3. If you're still not sure, then talk to a spiritual director, clergy person, or friend who understands the mystery of the call into darkness. Such a person should be able to help you discern the truth.

4. Let go. Let God. You cannot control the darkness. There is no exercise or formula or practice to perform that will get you through it or out of it.

5. Sit with God anyway, and be willing to wait for Him. When it's time, consolation will return. Paradoxically, you will both yearn to be out of the darkness and desire for it to never end. Hard to believe, huh?

When you emerge from the darkness, you'll discover that you have changed. The rough edges will have become smooth. The character defects will have given way to character assets. You will find that changes that began to occur in you, even before you began to willingly seek to know and do God's will, are now more noticeable and have begun to feel authentic. This deepening knowledge of yourself helps you to appraise yourself honestly and to see your good points and your shortcomings. You have truly begun to accept yourself exactly as you are. Now, you will be able to make progress toward becoming more like the true gold standard, which, of course, is God. You have made greater strides in replacing ego with humility, and you are now beginning to understand, with great awe, that you have achieved none of this on your own. Of ourselves, we are nothing. God does the work.

Sometimes we need help in emerging from the darkness. We feel lost and alone. We miss God but we can't seem to find our way back to the light. If this is true of you, don't despair. Counseling is available for your relationship with God. It's called spiritual direction.

Chapter 9

Fixing It, or Can We Get Counseling?

*D*uring that time when I had gone from God being the primary relationship of my life to profound feelings of emptiness—the sense of loss was extreme—I began to experience an underlying sadness that coated my spirit with heaviness and darkness. I felt bereft, alone, and lonely.

I knew from reading and study that this state of being wasn't unusual, even for people who had had deep, mystical, or life-transforming encounters with the Divine. John of the Cross, Teresa of Avila, C. S. Lewis, Thomas Merton, Martin Luther, and AA's co-founder Bill Wilson all had periods of devastating darkness. I understood that prayer and emptiness were both gifts from God calling us closer to Him.

I thought to myself, *If I could just know that I'm going through a dark night of the soul, like the mystics and other deeply spiritual people do, rather than a temper tantrum because I didn't get what I wanted, I could accept that.*

Was this more spiritual pride, wanting to be counted among the spiritual giants? Was I angling for knowledge that I was being singled out by God for my spiritual specialness?

Mostly I believed I was having a childish rebellion. If I tried hard enough, found the correct prayer ritual, or spoke to the right person who would have just the right words, I'd snap out of it. It didn't happen that way. In fact, it took years until I let go of my anger and lack of trust.

During that period, I often compared my relationship with God to that of a married couple who had a devastating argument. The wife got very upset because her husband hadn't given her what she wanted and believed she deserved. She couldn't understand why he hadn't, and she stopped trusting him. She moved into the living room and slept on the couch where it was cold and uncomfortable. She stubbornly stayed out there night after night, week after week, and month after month. She knew her husband loved her and was waiting for her to come back to his warm and loving arms where she would feel safe again. He would wait faithfully but never force himself upon her.

This wounded woman held out long past all reason. She held out until she could hardly remember the sting she felt when she had first moved out, and the seemingly unbearable losses had long been replaced with new hope and direction.

Sometimes this scenario proceeds all the way to moving out of the house or even divorce. This happens when all faith and belief have been lost, often because church leadership or the community itself has let you down or because you believe your behavior has been beyond pardon. Sometimes this happens because you feel that God Himself has let you down.

If you're someone who once had faith and then lost it, you may be experiencing a terrible emptiness that nothing can fill. No person, no job, no money, no success, no substance, no other obsession will do. Grief for God or church may overwhelm you, but you probably won't even have language or insight to grasp what's going on.

What a miserable and lonely place to be.

The good news is that God is not human. People are. So are you. Church leadership and community are made up of fallible folks like us. God always wants you back, and if you're willing to try, He'll help you find a way to move back in and recover the trust that has been so damaged or lost.

God Doesn't Close One Door without Opening Another; It's the Hallway Between That's So Dark

After the door slammed shut on my plans to stay in the navy, my spiritual life turned into five years of aimless wandering. As my loneliness for God deepened, I sought out Father Terry, a priest acquaintance who was off-the-charts smart and had a great sense of humor and awareness of his own human foibles. I knew he would understand me and not judge me. He might even have some wisdom or good advice to offer. We talked for awhile and when I left, I remembered little of what he had said. What stuck with me was one part of our conversation: "You seem to feel like God betrayed you, let you down on a promise He made."

I probably nodded my head vigorously at this observation, offered in Father Terry's understated, droll manner. Someone had finally put words to my feelings.

"Why don't you pray every day for God to heal your deep sense of betrayal?" he suggested. "And keep it up until your anger is gone."

I did this faithfully for a long time, perhaps several months or a year. Then one day—I don't know exactly when or how it happened—I became aware that it had been removed. I was no longer angry. I was no longer the wounded victim of betrayal by my Beloved.

But I had not yet reached the end of the dark hallway. Anger had been replaced by complacency and indifference. I had no desire to pray. I was numb. I just didn't care anymore. Yet that must not have been completely true, because I continued, as always, believing, acting faithfully, and speaking of God to others.

I felt like one of my limbs had been amputated. I got along without it and managed to live my life with a large degree of normalcy. But from time to time, I experienced intense phantom pain, as if the limb were still there. When that happened, I talked about my relationship with God, or apparent lack of it, to anyone who would listen. Tears would spring to my eyes, my voice would quiver with the pain, but my heart wouldn't melt. No one seemed to have an answer.

I went to church, and my mind wandered. I left unfilled, bored. I thought perhaps this was spiritual warfare, but I was neither impassioned nor emboldened enough to battle. I read C. S. Lewis's *Screwtape Letters,* a humorous but telling description of how the devil tempts us and deludes us. It neither convinced nor motivated me.

On and on I went with no apparent spiritual change of heart. Well, that's not quite the case. Alternating periods of complacency and intense sadness slowly gave way to some willingness to talk to God.

For a while, I carried around an old green, no longer functioning cordless phone receiver and went through the motions of "phoning" God, talking to Him and trying to listen. I dialed 1-800-GOD-HELP.

"Hi, God. This is Judith. Oh, You recognized my voice? I know it's been a long time, but listen, my secretary is quitting. I owe four thousand dollars in taxes, and I have no idea where I'm going to get the money. My daughter's having trouble with her boyfriend. I can't handle it all myself, but I'm not sure I can trust You to take care of it. What should I do, God? Are You even listening? What? Huh? You say I should quiet down. It will all work out. Wait and see. Okay, God. I'll try. Got to go. I'm really tired. Good night. Yes, I'll call again."

I talked to people who made all kinds of suggestions—books for me to read, excursions into the woods or to the ocean to find God in nature, various methods of prayer, words to repeat, and acts of service to perform. I tried all of these, but none of them stuck. I was unable or unwilling to be consistent or to bring anything to completion.

Then one day I was in excruciating pain from what turned out to be a gall bladder attack. I went to urgent care for treatment and came home that night with antibiotics and a determination to talk to the Divine Physician. I couldn't get comfortable. I couldn't sleep. I felt like the pain was going to go on forever. It was the middle of the night, and I didn't want to bother any of my friends, though I knew I could if I absolutely needed to. I knew I had to take it a minute at a time, and I didn't think I could do this alone.

So I gave in. I wrote a long letter to God telling Him what was going on in my life, my mind, and my heart. I begged for help. Almost instantly, I felt some relief from both the physical and the spiritual pain. I was granted the gift of willingness to continue writing, and I have written a letter to God every night since then, more than five years by now. My letters have varied in intensity and purpose.

- They have sometimes been full of superficial, "Dear Diary, this is what happened today" kinds of stuff.
- Sometimes they have been an examination of conscience, in which I confessed my shortcomings or failures to God, asking for help to do better, or I have identified the moments when God has been most present or most absent during that day.
- Often my letters have been celebration and thanksgiving when I've done something right or for the many gifts in my life.
- At times, they have been requests for guidance and knowledge of God's will for me in any given situation.
- And sometimes they have been requests for divine intervention for people I love, for my patients, for victims of natural disasters, or for world peace.

These letters were an essential part of the path through the dark hallway, the road back to a relationship with God. However, I was willing only to talk, not to listen. And trust remained tentative and conditional, far from surrender.

Finally, after another five years of stumbling through the dark and seemingly deserted hallway, the other door opened. I went to a New Year's weekend retreat at the same place where, years earlier, I had first hung out with God and discovered that I was never really alone.

I cornered Father Hanley, one of the priests working at the retreat house. One more time, expecting nothing, I told my whole sad story of having lost God.

Father Hanley listened intently, and then said, "You sound like a woman in a long-term marriage where the communication has gone stale. Maybe you should consider trying spiritual direction again."

It had been ten long years since I had shut down to God. Yet, just like that, I began to thaw in earnest. I don't know why. I had been writing my letters to God for almost a year, and I guess I had become ready to hear those words.

Spiritual direction had helped me many years before. Maybe it would help again now. Father Hanley helped me to locate a spiritual director close to my home.

It had been a long way back to God for me. The question of whether that period of time was a dark night of the soul imposed by God to bring me closer to Him or a prolonged temper tantrum had become irrelevant. What was important was that I made it through the long, dark hallway, and I found myself renewed and full of hope as I stepped through the now opened door.

When the Pupil Is Ready, the Teacher Will Appear

Thirty years ago, when I decided to stop looking for God in all the wrong places, a teacher was provided. That was Ruthie, the woman who became my second mother. She was wise and honest and trustworthy. She taught me how to live, since I had apparently not learned that lesson very well when I was growing up.

As I was trying to get to know God, many people, including Ruthie, who later became my spiritual mentor, began to teach me what they knew about God. Within months of the start of my spiritual journey, I decided to pursue instruction in the Catholic faith. Since childhood, I had been drawn toward this religious tradition. God knew that I was vulnerable, somewhat suggestible, and needed a flexible teacher. He provided me with Father Anton, who also became my friend and a guide into my new faith.

When I needed the right words of wisdom to get me back on track, Father Terry and Father Hanley appeared for a brief moment of time to say the very thing that I needed to hear. They were like bookends for my healing, one starting the process and one helping me to emerge into the light. So it has been throughout my life since I've come to know God.

Once I made the decision to recommit to my relationship with God by entering spiritual direction, I had a deep knowing that this was the right thing to do. I began to feel better almost immediately. Why I had to travel five hundred miles for a New Year's retreat to hear what Father Hanley had to say, I don't know.

It's entirely possible that had someone offered the very same suggestion at any other point in time, I might not have listened or been willing to act on the advice.

But here I was, two months later, knocking on the door of the Holistic Healing Center for my first visit with Sister Eileen. I didn't know what to expect other than a woman who owned the jolly voice and decidedly Irish accent that I'd heard on the phone. The door opened, and I was greeted by a slender, six-foot-tall woman with soft white hair, twinkling eyes, and a face free of wrinkles. She was wearing a conservative blue suit, a white blouse, and low-heeled, practical shoes. She didn't look anything like my idea of a nun, not that I had much notion of what one would look like!

Sister Eileen's strong presence came from her aura of serenity and her ability to be totally present in the moment. She seemed to invite God's presence into the room and into our relationship, helping me to feel safe. She listened to me intently as I shared with her my experience of God in my life. I had not only walked through the door into a new relationship with a spiritual guide, but I had also knocked on God's door, where He had been waiting for a long time, patiently and expectantly, to welcome me home.

My arrival at Sister Eileen's door was the signal that I was willing not only to pray (talk to God) but also to meditate, which meant listening. With this wise and loving woman as my guide and partner in discerning God's will in my life, changes in my relationship with God began to occur.

When I arrived at my appointments with Sister Eileen, she would often start the hour with a reading from scripture. I don't know how she did it (probably by quieting down and listening to the Holy Spirit before our sessions), but she always seemed to pick the perfect passage for me.

On one occasion, she chose the story about the apostles being out on their boat when they saw Jesus walking toward them on the lake. They became frightened, thinking they were seeing a ghost. Jesus told them not to be afraid, and when Peter challenged Him, He invited Peter to come to Him by walking on the water himself. Peter started out just fine, making some headway before he panicked and started to sink. He begged Jesus to save him, and, of course, "Jesus reached out His hand and caught him," saying, "You of little faith. Why did you doubt?"

Immediately, this story became a metaphor for my journey of the past few years. In prayer, I asked Jesus to rescue me. Almost immediately, I sensed Him saying to me, *"Judith, you were doing so well and had great faith. Why did you doubt me?"* I then felt Him reach out His hand and bring me into His arms. Sister Eileen pointed out that I had begun to allow Him to restore my faith and my trust.

During another meeting, Sister Eileen began with the story about the disciples getting terrified when a huge storm began rocking their boat. Jesus was sleeping, but they woke Him up to tell Him they were about to drown. Jesus then commanded the wind and the surf to be still. "Why are you so afraid? Do you still have so little faith?"

At that time, my daughter was finally starting to rebel. I had somehow thought that because of our closeness, I would be spared having to go through the pain and uncertainty that comes when your beloved child begins to falter. After Sister Eileen read this passage, I again began to pray.

I found myself telling Jesus that I felt like I was about to drown in my feelings of dread for my daughter. "Jesus, don't You even care? Why don't You do something about what's happening here?" Again, I felt as if He were holding me, and some of the fear began to go away.

Sister Eileen commented, "He might not change what your daughter is doing because she hasn't asked, but He sure seems to be changing your reactions to her so that you can weather the stormy seas ahead."

At another point in my life, a trainer at the gym asked me how I was doing. I paused a moment, not knowing what to say. I had the sudden realization that whenever I was asked how I was, I answered by telling what my daughter was doing. The thing was that I didn't want to say what was going on with my daughter. I didn't think she was doing very well, so I was left speechless. Suddenly, I had the overpowering realization that I had better get a life of my own.

The next time I met with Sister Eileen, I told her about this insight and how much at a loss I was about where to even start. As usual, she suggested that I take it to God in prayer. After quieting down a bit, I began describing the situation to God and asking for guidance. I began to think about the disciples and how Jesus went around picking them. They would drop what they were doing and follow Him. So I imagined having a conversation with Peter.

"Peter, I don't know what to do."

His reply was, *Now that you have more time to pursue an interest of yours, what would it be?*

"I don't know. Something having to do with God, I suppose. I'm always talking about God to my patients, but I can't make Him the full focus of the counseling."

Peter just smiled and said, *I know you'll find a way.* That was all.

I reported this to Sister Eileen and told her that I'd been interested in leading spiritual retreats for a long time. Perhaps some training as a spiritual director would help me accomplish this. I was afraid, when it came down to it, I wouldn't have the words to say. I told her, "I don't feel smart enough or wise enough."

She just smiled and commented, "I don't think that the apostles were chosen for their intelligence or wisdom. It was for their faith and willingness to give themselves to Jesus."

With that permission and the fact that she didn't just laugh, I began to seek training as a spiritual director.

With the help of Sister Eileen's wise counsel, a result of her trust in God's presence, and her ability to listen for His guidance, my communication with God came first with great effort, a mere trickle of water beneath the desert sand. Over time, trust once again began to grow, and the trickle became a stream of clear, fresh water. Communication became more and more open and honest.

God and I were partners again.

Spiritual Direction—How to Get Counseling with God

A spiritual director is a loving companion who helps to provide a safe, secure space in which you can explore the relationship between any aspect of your inner or outer life and God. The real director is God's loving presence working through both you and your spiritual guide. You don't have to be a saint or a mystic to enter spiritual direction. You don't need to be walking on water or have a high IQ or be a pillar of your religious or church community. The only requirement is a desire to be closer to God and to try, as best you can, to live your life according to His will for you.

Here are some reasons why you might choose to seek spiritual direction. You may have

- a desire to draw closer to God or to know Him better
- a longing to live out of your deepest center where the Divine resides
- a yearning for a richer, more contemplative prayer life
- a thirst for knowledge of God's will in your everyday life
- a need for spiritual guidance in making an important or life-changing decision, such as discerning a vocation for ministry, getting married, or changing jobs or career

Your reasons for seeking spiritual direction may be emotional in nature. Perhaps you have

- doubts about whether God really knows what he's doing in your life, your family, the community, or the world
- a loss of the sense of meaning in your life
- a sense of woundedness that needs healing
- a feeling of emptiness or darkness that may be frightening or confusing and is accompanied by an inability to pray
- a readiness to confront your shadow (the hidden side of your nature, which we all have), addressing its effects on your life, including sin, character shortcomings, lack of balance, and negative emotions

Spiritual direction will also be helpful to you if you are

- wanting guidance, experience, or expertise as you embark on your spiritual journey
- seeking instruction in how to pray or meditate
- doubting your faith, doctrine, church leadership, or place in your community

Many spiritual directors have received formal training that has led to a certificate or degree. However, in some circumstances, life experience may be the main qualification. For instance, a priest, pastor, rabbi, or other person in an established religious ministry or vocation may serve as a spiritual director.

In less formalized communities, such as Twelve Step self-help groups, your sponsor may serve as your spiritual guide. Informal spiritual directors are often found on your life path: parents, grandparents, godparents, friends, and teachers.

Experience alone does not qualify an individual to take on this role. Such a person should also have qualities of personality, character, and faith to fill the shoes of a spiritual guide and mentor. In choosing the right person to fill this role, you might want to consider the kind of person who would make you feel most comfortable, someone you could come to trust completely. This is important because you may be sharing difficult, painful, sometimes embarrassing or humiliating thoughts or experiences. If you feel that you will have trouble talking to someone of the opposite sex, seek a director of the same sex. If you're more comfortable sharing with someone who is grandfatherly because you had wonderful experiences with your grandparent, then look for someone who will fit that bill. If you need a person who is particularly nurturing or motherly because your mom died at an early age or was absent for other reasons, then look for that trait. Above all, ask God to help you find the right person to fill this sensitive but powerful role in your life.

What qualities should you look for in a spiritual director? Of foremost importance is finding someone whose spirituality is the central organizing principle of his or her life. There are some other qualities you might look for. Your director should be an individual who

- is further ahead in the spiritual journey than you are
- receives direction for his or her own continued personal growth and an ever-deepening relationship with God
- is a prayerful person with strong moral values who is seriously motivated to live a godly life and takes action on a daily basis to do so

- has had deep, contemplative prayer experiences and understands the various peaks and pitfalls of serious prayer life, including experiences of darkness, emptiness, or difficulty in prayer
- studies and lives according to the written precepts of his or her chosen spiritual or religious path

Your guide in this important pursuit should also have skills and sufficient self-knowledge to help you along this rewarding but often challenging path. The qualified director

- is not afraid of strong feelings, including love, passion, fear, anger, doubt, confusion, and emptiness, and is not uncomfortable listening to another's sometimes gritty life experience
- has some understanding of psychology, personality, and the unconscious life
- is mature, with sound judgment and wisdom that comes from life experience
- is empathic, nonjudgmental, sincere, and without personal agenda
- desires to help you discover God's will in your life without giving advice or pushing a particular point of view

• • •

The practice of spiritual direction stems from the time of the early Christian hermits (300–400 A.D.) who sought to follow the Old Testament spirituality of withdrawing alone into the desert, where they lived their lives immersed in prayer. They were men and women who were believed to be wise contemplatives with a deeply mystical connection to the Divine. Clergy and monastics often sought them out for spiritual guidance.

Spiritual direction flourished in the Roman Catholic tradition, with greater formalization in the Jesuit, Benedictine, and Franciscan religious communities. It was also deeply embedded in Sufism, the Islamic mystical tradition. It was only during the latter half of the twentieth century that Protestant and Jewish faith communities began to embrace spiritual direction as an accepted method of deepening a relationship with God and with their faith traditions.

Another modern form of spiritual direction can be found in the Twelve Step tradition. An Alcoholics Anonymous (AA) sponsor functions as an informal spiritual director by using the Twelve Steps to help individuals to stay sober, have a spiritual experience, achieve humility through deeper self-knowledge, and seek knowledge of God's will through prayer and meditation.

• • •

What can you expect to experience once you have found the right director? Each director will have an individualized approach to the process based on the director's training, life experience, personal experience of direction, personality, religion, or spiritual approach. What all Judeo-Christian and Islamic direction have in common are the central goals of exploring and discerning the presence of the Divine in your life, becoming open to God in all things and all experiences, and deepening the practice of your spiritual traditions, personally as well as in your family and faith community.

Usually spiritual direction occurs on a monthly basis, at an office or other predetermined location with an agreed-upon fee. Sometimes there is no fee. While you and your director are equals before God, a degree of professional distance and role boundaries are maintained in order to preserve neutrality and openness in discerning God's will. Your director will usually provide an informal contract defining what spiritual direction is, along with expectations regarding frequency, place, amount of time, cost, and roles. There will also generally be a proviso that states that spiritual direction is not psychotherapy, pastoral counseling, or religious education. It is not aimed at solving problems or fixing personality or teaching communication skills.

In some instances, you'll have a contract that is verbal and general in nature. This is especially true if your relationship is an informal one, such as sponsorship in a Twelve Step program. In all cases, you and your director, mentor, sponsor, or guide should evaluate the relationship and process after an agreed-upon period of time to be sure your needs are being adequately and appropriately met. There's no reason why you or even your director can't choose to end the relationship if it isn't working out.

Often a spiritual direction session will begin with prayer, spiritual reading, or a period of silence. You might share what you experienced during this initial prayer time. Then, if this is your first meeting, you will have an opportunity to talk about yourself, why you are seeking spiritual direction, what your relationship with God and your prayer life has been like, what questions you have about the spiritual direction process, and what you'd like to know about the spiritual director.

If you agree to continue the process, then the following sessions might also start with reading and silent or spoken prayer. You will then talk about what has gone on in your life during the previous month and where God has been present. You might share your prayer experiences, what God seems to be communicating or asking of you, what difficulties you've had, and what questions or feelings have arisen.

Your director might ask questions to clarify what you are saying and to be sure you feel understood. You might be asked to take something to God in prayer right then. Your director will be seeking divine guidance while you are sharing or praying. Drawing on training and experience, your director will help you discern when you're moving toward God or away from Him, or what He might be calling you to do. The session may also end in prayer.

There are many resources for finding a spiritual director:

1. Ask friends about their directors.
2. Ask at your church, prayer group, or AA meeting. It may not be a good idea to ask someone familiar to you—your parish priest, pastor, church ministry leader, rabbi, family member, or friend—to fill this role because the information shared is often very private and personal. You might feel uncomfortable sharing so intimately one day and sitting on a church committee or at the dinner table the next day. Also, switching from one role to the other might prove

to be a conflict for the director, who has to uphold church doctrine on one occasion and be an understanding, accepting spiritual counselor the next.

3. Ask at local retreat centers or other spiritual ministries.
4. Inquire at the religion or pastoral counseling departments of colleges or universities that are connected with a religious organization.
5. Ask at schools that offer certificates or degrees in spiritual direction.
6. Go online. Google "spiritual direction" or name the specific religious or spiritual path in which you want direction, such as "Christian spiritual direction," and you will be led to a wealth of information.
7. Other online resources include these:
   a. Christian Formation and Direction Ministries (cfdm .org)
   b. Christos Center for Spiritual Direction (christoscenter .org)
   c. Spiritual Directors International, an ecumenical organization of spiritual directors from all spiritual/ religious paths (sdiworld.org)
   d. Yedidya Center for Jewish Spiritual Direction (yedidyacenter.org)
   e. Franciscan Friars Third Order Regular (franciscan friarstor.com)

Leading a spiritual life is a never-ending adventure, a process and journey that continues to produce rich fruit. Your relationship with God has, by now, matured. You are comfortable with Him, and you are prepared, even excited, about continuing your life with God always at your side.

Chapter 10

Our Relationship Improves, or Mature Partnership

A pastor teaching about sustaining successful marriage relationships recommended a talk a day, a date a week, and something special together once a month. I have often recommended this simple formula to couples in counseling to keep communication and romance in the relationship and to build couple strength, from which everything flows in a family.

I have adopted this routine, not just to maintain, but also to enrich and enliven my relationship with God. We have brief contacts throughout the day. "God, I meant to tell You that . . . God, what do You think I should do about . . . ? God, thanks for helping me through . . . God, I'm so tired, so thirsty, so in need of a break, so glad I got that done."

These quick check-ins don't take the place of the talk a day. That's our prayer and meditation time, which, for me, takes place every evening before bed. A specific time reserved for this daily communication is of crucial importance.

Then there is the date each week. For me, this could be going to church, taking a walk in the woods, listening to music, writing or reading about spiritual topics, going to a museum, or even sitting in my favorite coffee shop with a café americano. Our date could be any activity, as long as I have invited God to join me or He is taking me somewhere by way of inspiration or spontaneity.

Once every month or two, I try to do something special with God. This could be a day or weekend retreat, structured or not, a class, individual or group spiritual direction, hanging out with a God-centered friend, or participating in a ministry.

As these activities have become a natural part of my life, I find that my relationship with God flows comfortably. We are more like an old married couple who are at ease with one another and confident in their love. It doesn't require constant analysis or second-guessing about motives or methods. We can talk or be quiet, laugh or cry. I know God is there for me no matter what. He's a friend who is on my side. He is as close to me as my own skin, totally part of me and my consciousness.

Love Is an Action

I can't count the number of times patients have come to me saying, "I love him (or her), but I'm just not *in love* anymore." They come from the hooked-on-the-feelings school of thought. When the passion cools, there can't be love, right?

Wrong!

As love matures, it becomes faithful action and commitment. It's being kind, honest, humble, generous, supportive, and affectionate. It's being respectful and understanding. It's being accepting of the opinions and values of your loved one even if they are different from yours. These are the attitudes that fill a loving home and provide a safe and secure environment in which to raise a family.

It's true that without the thrill and excitement that occurs in the early stages of a relationship, the human race might have died out long ago. But it's when the initial thrill is gone that the wonderful, but often difficult, journey begins.

I finally accepted that a good relationship with God could not be measured by the presence or absence of strong emotions. His love wasn't conditional on my being a good girl. I didn't have to be, feel, believe, think, or act any particular way to gain His love. And just maybe God didn't have to be, feel, believe, think, or act any particular way to gain my love; we had a deal!

Here's how I try to show my love for God each day. I'm not a morning person, so I don't pretend that I am. God knows better anyway. So, I say, "Good morning, God." That's about all He gets from me before I'm dressed and on my way. At any rate, I had put today in His hands before I went to sleep the previous night. I talk about God throughout the day to patients, friends, and co-workers. When I get a break during the day, I take a few minutes to quiet down and acknowledge Him. I try to take care of my body each day, since He lives within me. By this, I mean that I try to eat right, exercise, and get enough rest, though many days I fall short. I try to recognize God in others and let that knowledge be reflected in my behavior. I thank God when good things happen. I ask for help when I'm confused, anxious, or angry. I recognize God in small things, especially in coincidences (which have been called minor miracles in which God chooses to remain anonymous). I honor God by putting in a full day's work for a full day's pay. I try to be responsible, reliable, trustworthy, kind, caring, loving, honest, and open. Our time together in prayer comes at the end of the day. I try to be open to God's ideas, urgings, and ways.

I know these behaviors and attitudes please Him. I no longer think that if I can't feel God's presence, He must not be there. I no longer believe that if life isn't going according to my plan, it's God's fault and I should withdraw my trust as an act of self-defense. I no longer believe that if I'm having a bad patch emotionally, physically, financially, occupationally, socially, or with family or friends that I'm being punished or that I'm failing in some way. In other words, just because I don't like something in my life, it doesn't mean I'm not praying enough or the right way.

I know that God is present in all things, in every aspect of my life, in the apparent good and in the apparent bad. If I keep trying to express my love for Him in action, thought, word, and attitude, I know that God will be well pleased, and He will know that He is well loved. My life will reflect our unbreakable commitment to love.

The Gateway to Grace Is Gratitude

Growing up as I did in a Jewish home, I have no idea where I got the notion of a fall from grace. But got it I did. I would worry that if I did this one thing, God would be upset with me, and I would fall from grace. Then I would inevitably do it, and it would then become easier and easier each time. Then the one most awful thing would be replaced with another. And before long, I would do that too, setting myself up for another fall from grace. First it would be getting drunk; then it would be getting drunk during the day. Then it would be maxing out a credit card; and then getting a second card; then obtaining a consolidation loan; then adding more debt, starting the cycle over. It seemed like I could never get it right in my own eyes or in God's. So I continually had the feeling of being one minute or one misstep away from going down the proverbial tubes.

When I was a kid, my mom would tell me, "Only the people who love you will tell you the truth." Then she'd lay one of her truths on me, and I'd be out for the round. I always thought she was judging me. I guess that was my first sense of a fall from grace.

Many years later, I was very concerned about a close friend. I thought she was taking some actions that would harm her and that seemed contradictory to the things I thought she believed in. I wasn't judging her; I was genuinely worried. So I decided to tell her. She felt judged by me, and I lost that friendship. What I gained in the process was the knowledge that my mother wasn't being either judgmental or rejecting. She was trying to save me, in her way, from trouble and hurt. Perhaps I would've been able to grasp that if her criticism had been balanced with approval.

After she died, my dad told me that my mom bragged about me every chance she got. *So why didn't she tell me?* I wanted to know. *Did she somehow think I knew?*

My mother apparently also asked my dad with great hurt, "What have I done that she hates me so much?" The answer was simple: she never told me she loved me. She never cheered me on. She never let me in on the secret that she was proud of me. She didn't know how to express her love.

During marital counseling, how often I hear, "You never tell me you love me."

How common is the answer, "You know I love you. Why do I have to tell you?"

These comments occur over and over among couples who come to me for help. There is no ESP in relationships. You can't assume that your spouse, lover, parent, or child just knows. It can't be left to guesswork. It has to be said often and acted upon in ways that leave little or no room for doubt.

When is the last time you acknowledged your spouse, your child, your friend, your boss, your parents, or God for doing something right, something you appreciated? It seems that in everyday life, we can count on receiving criticism but rarely get approval. In the classic book on management *The One Minute Manager,* bosses are told to regularly catch their employees doing something right and tell them.

Approval and recognition are motivating. Being ignored or continuously criticized is demoralizing. So why is it that we are so stingy with encouragement of those closest to us? We get lazy, self-centered. We think others should be able to read our minds. We take people for granted. Or, like my mom, we just don't know how. No one ever modeled these attitudes for us.

A wife asks her husband to buy her some flowers or take her to dinner once in a while. But when he does, does she act appreciative? A mother asks her teenager to help out in the kitchen or pick up the clothes that are constantly left around. Does she think that because he's the kid and this is his responsibility there is no reason to acknowledge his efforts? Or if the job isn't done just right, does the teenager get a complaint or a correction without comment on having made an effort? A husband wants his wife to greet him with a smile when he gets home from work and give him thirty minutes to decompress before she begins running down her day's complaints. After doing this, does he say, "That really helped, honey. Now, how did your day go?"

Besides looking at what's wrong, do we look for what's right? Some days, all I can see is the negative. Then I find myself depressed or full of self-pity. I'm upset about the seven-hundred-dollar brake job required on my one-year-old car, forgetting to be grateful that I have the money to pay for it. I'm annoyed that three patients were no-shows today, not remembering that I'm relieved that I now have time to write a report I otherwise would have had to take home over the weekend. I'm afraid no one will buy this book, not taking time to be awed by the fact that God has given me the knowledge, experience, and ability to write it. I've focused on lack instead of abundance, and I've gotten the results to match.

Early in our relationship, my friend and mentor Ruthie taught me that the best cure for self-pity, situational depression, or anger is gratitude. Whenever I whined about something, she would remind me to have an attitude of gratitude. When I was really in the pits, completely caught up in the negative, she would tell me to write a gratitude list.

> *Thank you, God, for allowing me to wake up this morning, for my health, my child, my dogs and cats, my home, my friends, my job, the grass, the trees, the flowers, and the sky.*

I can't tell you how much I disliked writing this list when I was having such a good pity party. Sometimes I chose to remain in the funk I was in. But eventually, I gave in, wrote the list, and rather miraculously felt better.

These days, when I go for a walk, I often have a gratitude fest, listing for God all the things there are to be grateful for. Sometimes, I can keep it up for my entire half-hour walk. When I practice gratitude regularly, I'm better able to shift away from anger, fear, anxiety, or sadness when these emotions threaten to overwhelm me. I simply acknowledge the feeling, then focus on something I'm grateful for. Gratitude melts away the negative emotions.

I think of grace as God's love and protection, which He freely gives to us. And the cultivation of an attitude of gratitude is surely the gateway to the experience of God's grace.

How to Live Life on an Even Keel

Living life on an even keel. What is that?

I had gotten so used to life as a roller-coaster ride that peace and calm seemed like something must be wrong—weird and boring. Adrenaline had become a drug of choice for me. It accompanied anger, worry, and fear. It was sometimes exhilarating, sometimes exhausting, always dramatic and problematic.

Living life on life's terms was not part of my repertoire. I was always judging reality as good or bad, acceptable or not. I was rarely satisfied, always looking for something more, something different, something better.

I didn't trust myself; I didn't trust God. I was chronically afraid of making a mistake, being wrong. Moments of peace were actually the disguised eye of the hurricane. The stormy winds were always about to knock me off balance or sweep me up in their vortex, only to drop me later, bruised and bleeding. And worse yet, if no life disaster presented itself, I might stir one up, sabotaging any chance of success because I was so afraid of trying and failing.

There are many ways to sidestep peace and abundance. Drama isn't the only way. Some people passively make a mess through avoidance. They sleep or read or watch TV or spend hours alone in the garage tinkering. They go through life in a coma because it's safe. Others get so caught up in being aggressive and being right that they alienate themselves from anyone who would be close and supportive. Still others get focused on fixing and helping others, worrying about satisfying the needs or desires of family, friends, co-workers, even total strangers. They pour themselves out in community projects, trying to fix, improve, or beautify everything they are involved with. Their problems stem from ignoring themselves, becoming estranged from their own feelings, motivations, and desires. Many create chaos in their lives and relationships by an inability to make any decisions or by being so caught up in their thoughts or intellect that they don't connect to the people in their lives. Or they live in fantasy, preferring it to mundane reality.

Each of us develops a unique style of defensiveness. Whatever our method of self-protection, the end result is an inability to have a fulfilling life. We have to face our own truths and come to know and accept ourselves, our emotions, character assets, and shortcomings, so that we can live fully, love deeply, work meaningfully, give freely, serve willingly.

Much of this book has been aimed at helping you know

yourself and know God. It is my hope that following many of the suggestions that have been presented will result in your forming a strong partnership with God, that you will experience comfort with God, trusting Him and yourself to live each day in peace and acceptance.

Here are some activities to help you live life on an even keel, knowing that you are living God's plan for you:

1. Start each day by placing yourself in God's kind and loving care. Tell Him you are reporting in for duty, and ask Him for knowledge of His will for you for the day ahead.

2. Review the day ahead. Tell God that these are the things you think you need to accomplish. Ask God to help you get done the things that He wants you to, even if His list doesn't turn out to be the same as yours.

3. Spend some time each day in prayer and meditation (speaking and listening to God). Try to make this a daily set appointment with God that you always keep.

4. Do your best each day to do the things you like yourself for doing and avoid the things that you would dislike yourself for doing. In this way, you'll not only come to like yourself, but you'll put your head on the pillow at night knowing that you have pleased God.

5. When problems come up during the day, check in with God, asking for advice or guidance. Look and listen for God's presence and help throughout the day. It might come through a coincidence or something that someone says to you or that you read. It might be your gut intuition, the still small voice within, that you wisely decide to honor.

6. Take care of your body, God's dwelling place. Eat right, exercise, and get enough rest. Follow the orders of both your human and your divine physician.

7. Don't keep secrets. If something is going on in your thoughts or your life, current or past, that you're ashamed of or know is not good for you but you want to keep doing, share it with God and another person. Don't share your secret with someone who would be hurt by it. Keeping secrets will make you sick.

8. Develop an attitude of gratitude. Frequently review the things that you are grateful for and express your gratitude to people in your life and to God.

9. When you are troubled by your feelings, actions, or thoughts and you are caught up in selfishness or self-centeredness, find someone else you can help. Be of service in some way that will get your mind off of you.

10. Take care of yourself. Be as kind and loving toward yourself as you are toward others. This is the essence of the teaching "Love your neighbor as yourself."

11. Before you go to sleep, thank God for the day that has just ended. Review your thoughts, words, actions, and attitudes of the past twenty-four hours. Acknowledge what you have done right, and ask God for help in doing better. Make amends if you have fallen short.

12. Remember that reality is neither good nor bad. It just is. It's how you react to it or what you do with it that will make the difference.

By following these steps on a regular basis, by integrating them into my life, I have found that my life is filled with hope, peace, meaning, love, and abundance. I have a good time for the right reasons and have no need to stir up trouble for myself or anyone else.

With God's help, I have spent years laying the spiritual keel of my lifeboat. It has become my foundation and my structure, providing stability, keeping me afloat in spite of any gale force winds that blow into my life. No matter how ragged I get around the edges, my keel is secure, and I know I'll be okay.

Now that you're filled to overflowing with God's grace, you might experience a deep desire to share your joy with others. It is time to extend yourself charitably by offering service to your spiritual community.

Chapter 11

Sharing God in Community

I was longing for quiet time with just me and my God. I hadn't been on a silent retreat since my daughter was born, twenty-one years earlier. My dad had come to live with us shortly after her birth. Suddenly the quiet of my home was disrupted, and their needs took precedence over my wants. It was difficult to find time to be alone with God.

Recently, I was thrilled to have the opportunity to attend an eight-day silent retreat. There were sixty-two people sharing this experience, and we formed a community though we didn't exchange a single word. We prayed together, listened to inspirational talks, shared our meals, and smiled as we passed one another while wandering around the beautiful grounds of the retreat center.

Twenty-five years before, on my first silent retreat, I had no sense of the power of community because I was too wrapped up in myself, worrying about whether I was being appropriate, struggling with the absence of others' reactions to me, alternating between feeling noticeably out of place and fearing I was invisible like a hole in a doughnut. This time, my experience was remarkably different from that first time. I didn't notice this until halfway through.

Each day, we had the opportunity to participate, as a community, in centering prayer. Before lunch, anyone who desired to join in went to the chapel and listened to a few words of instruction regarding this method of prayer. The deep, mystical sound of a meditation gong seemed to signal my soul to quiet, and more than forty of the retreat participants settled down to twenty minutes of silence. We were taught to acknowledge the presence of each thought, sound, or physical sensation and then let it go. By saying a personally chosen sacred word, we refocused on the vast but somehow reassuring silence. The depth of peace that I experienced during these brief sessions was greater than anything I had encountered previously. It was as if our souls had become intertwined as they rose up in prayerful unison. Beyond words lies the Spirit of the universe that unites us as one in God.

What I realized then was that the power of the community in prayer far exceeded anything that I generally experience on my own. These fellow seekers of God's shelter and love were inextricably joined with me in our common desire to know Him more deeply.

I have often complained that my church community does not reach out to those of us who are divorced, widowed, unmarried, or single parents or who don't have traditional families. In the past, I used this as an excuse to stay away from church.

Since my retreat, I have greater respect for and understanding of the power and purpose of communal prayer. I desire and look forward to joining in prayer with others, and I know from experience that the power of prayer increases with the number of prayers. So I go to church to hear God's Word, to learn and to pray in community. But this does not excuse God's people from the responsibility of outreach, welcome, and hospitality to all who come as members of His family.

During the course of study for my certification as a spiritual director, I was given the assignment of writing my spiritual autobiography. This was a personal history of my relationship with God, including religion, influences, and changes in my path. It included times that I moved toward God or away from Him, periods of consolation or darkness, and variations in my degree of commitment to Him and His way of life. This autobiography was, in effect, a precursor to writing this book.

As I wrote, I began to realize the critical role that community played in the development of my relationship with God, my faith, and my spiritual life. I had, in fact, participated in many different religious or spiritually based groups that deeply influenced me but which I had never thought of as community.

The model for a spiritual community is the supportive family, led by loving parents, in which the children can learn to love God and one another. Each family member has importance and value as an individual and an important role within the family. However, because every child is different, a relationship is developed with each parent that reflects each child's unique personality.

As it is with our family, so it is with the community of God. He created us as social beings, meant to live and worship both at home with our family and in the larger spiritual community to which we are each led. And as with our experience in our family community, we each develop a different personal relationship with God. My relationship with my earthly father was significantly different from the relationships which my sister and brother had with him. Similarly, each of us, having been created by God, has a unique relationship with Him that reflects our own personality.

For many, the family is the first, and most obvious, spiritual community. This was not the case for me. Though there was love in my home, there was little or no talk of God. We spoke of religious holidays such as the Jewish New Year or occasions such as bar mitzvah. But we didn't speak of relationship with God, the meaning of scripture, our spiritual beliefs, or prayer.

Instead, I first encountered God at summer camp. I happily passed my sixth through my fourteenth birthdays at an eight-week sleepover camp for Jewish girls in the magnificent and majestic Adirondack Mountains near Saranac Lake, New York. Here I learned the spiritual peace and wonder of nature. I found this in the incense of the pine trees, the intensely blue skies with cotton clouds, the muted sound of rain falling on pine-covered paths, the power of electrical storms with streaks of lightning and rolling thunder, and the serene calm of the lake as our canoe paddles cut through the water.

Every Saturday, different groups of girls would be called upon to conduct Sabbath services. This was an honor and a joy that we took on with serious and careful attention. Here, I learned to appreciate the haunting minor-key melodies of the Jewish prayers, the comfort of tradition, and deep respect for God.

I attended Sunday school from first through tenth grade (confirmation), and in these classes, I learned Bible history, the role of the prophets, and the stories of the Old Testament. I loved these classes and the sense of belonging I felt in that community.

From childhood, I had been attracted to Christianity. I was glued to the TV at Easter each year, watching movies like *Barabbas* and *The Robe*. I was attracted to the loving personality of Jesus, and I wondered if He was the Son of God. When I traveled, I loved visiting cathedrals, and I was transported by medieval and Renaissance religious art. In college, I was turned down by Jewish sororities and rushed by the Christian ones. When I applied for graduate school, I was accepted by two Catholic schools, St. John's University and DePaul.

As an adult, I came to know God in a more personal way, encouraged by a wonderful group of wise women who taught me the value of discerning God's will and surrender. The love I found in this community was unparalleled. Through the unconditional acceptance of these women, I learned to know and trust God, myself, and others. They also encouraged me to pursue the Christian faith that I had been strongly attracted to throughout my life, not because they thought this was the only true or right way but because this is the way that I believed God was calling me.

I have treated many couples whose marital difficulties seem to stem from their isolating from the larger community and looking to one another to be the only friend, the only support, the only source of fulfillment. When this happens, the couple becomes a closed system. There is never outside input or experience except perhaps through work associates. The relationship begins to suffer from sepsis, a poison that cuts off the sunlight, fresh air, and water needed for new life.

When a relationship is healthy, each partner can move close to the other, experiencing deep friendship, intimacy, and pleasure in one another's company. But they also move into the community and enjoy outside friendships, pursue individual interests, and have other sources of fulfillment and self-esteem. In such a relationship, love so fills up each partner that it overflows, reaching outward to touch and interact with the world beyond the partnership.

So it should be in our relationship with God. We become so filled with His love and our love for Him that we feel compelled to share that love with others. We see God not only in our friends and extended family, but also in strangers, in the poor, the sick, the homeless, or less fortunate. We need to reach out, participate, and give service.

There are many different communities in which we can be nourished and through which we can contribute. At your place of worship, there are prayer groups and book studies based on the teachings of your chosen religion. There are committees to organize social events, to welcome newcomers, to raise money, or to serve the homebound of your religious or spiritual community. You could join the worship team or the choir, be one of the folks who decorate the chapel, temple, or mosque, or serve on the council that makes policy for your religious or spiritual organization.

In the neighborhood, people join together for social gatherings, as part of a safety team or neighborhood watch, or to raise funds for support of local arts. People might join together to watch one another's kids, plant the local park, plan walking or bike trails, or clean up graffiti.

Support groups are wonderful examples of God's people helping one another out. These include writing groups, Twelve Step groups, and groups to support people who are grieving, caregivers of the elderly, family members of the mentally ill, or patients recovering from cancer or other illnesses.

Spiritual direction groups are formed for people wanting to share the ways that God has been present in their daily lives, their prayer life, or their dreams and discern where the Spirit is leading them. They might desire to meditate together, share about their relationships with God, or heal broken trust with church or God.

Each of us is led by God to the community that is right for us. We only need to be open to His call to experience Him through our travels with others.

Pain Shared Is Cut in Half, and Joy Shared Is Doubled

In my family, we celebrated whatever holiday Hallmark Cards was celebrating. It rarely mattered what tradition was being honored. It just seemed that we liked a good reason to share a delicious meal.

As secular Jews, we shared the Sunday morning ritual of lox and bagels or the Sunday evening feast on deli food. Food and comfort became indelibly connected in my mind, as did food and celebration. If I was sick, I got nurturing food like mashed potatoes, rice pudding, or ice cream. If I was hurt, angry, or lonely, it might be chips or anything sweet.

Ah, but if we were celebrating, that was another thing altogether. There was corned beef and cabbage for Saint Paddy's Day, an entire seder meal at Passover, including charoset (an apple, nut, and date mix) and Matzoh Charlotte (a lemony, sweet dessert). For Purim, there were danish and hamantaschen, pastries shaped like the three-sided hat of the evil vizier Haman from the Book of Esther. For Easter, we ate delicious baked ham (!) and got a basket of goodies from the Easter bunny. In the summer, we were very American with barbeques and cookouts. In the fall, we had chopped liver, roast beef, mashed potatoes, and challah bread for the Jewish New Year, and we broke the Yom Kippur fast with blintzes, noodle kugel, whitefish, and any number of dairy treats. For Thanksgiving, of course, we had turkey with all the trimmings, and for Christmas, there were lox and bagels and pancakes in the morning (after we opened the presents Santa had left under the "Hanukkah bush") and a massive array of roast beef, ham, and turkey for dinner. For birthdays, the birthday person got to dictate the menu, including the kind of cake and ice cream that would be served.

What were we really celebrating with all that food at all those meals? I think we were feasting family and honoring tradition.

More important than food on occasions of sadness or joy were the people who held me and comforted me when I was in pain or who laughed with me and hugged me when life gave me success or satisfaction.

I remember my first devastating heartbreak. Rick was gorgeous to look at and exciting to be with. We went to college and partied together, and we were inseparable. But after graduation, our relationship became tumultuous, on again, off again. He was the first love of my life, and when the final breakup came, I thought life was over.

I called my big sister in the middle of the night and cried my eyes out. She listened, offered assurances, and just hung in there with me as long as I needed her to. I don't remember anything she said. I just remember the comfort of her listening presence.

As a senior in college, I was rush chairman for my sorority. Though I was Jewish, there was a definite bias toward Christianity in the national organization. One of the national sorority leaders came to support us that fall.

I was devastated when she said, "Judith, we want to see a strong rush season. But you should remember that Jews are welcome only as long as they are also Christian." *Whatever that meant!*

Jani was my best friend and one of my sorority sisters. She had grown up in South America with a Polish father and an Italian mother. She was brilliant, with statuesque European features and a great sense of humor, and was a dedicated and loyal friend. On the day that the representative from the sorority's national organization made that astonishing and devastating remark, Jani did something I will never forget, something she and I still talk about to this day.

She took off her sorority pin, threw it down, and walked out the front door of the sorority house, saying in a low but clear and menacing voice (amazing for this normally mild-mannered young woman), "If this is what this sorority is about, I'm not Christian, I'm not Jewish, and I'm certainly no longer a member of this organization."

With that, the other sisters followed suit, taking off their pins, throwing them down, and walking out, leaving the stunned woman from national behind, gaping in disbelief. It was not the first time I had experienced prejudice, and these courageous women held me and comforted me. And, oh yes, we mustn't forget the apology that came from the national headquarters and the fact that they no longer messed with our local membership.

At every painful moment in my life, I've always had someone to turn to. I'm fortunate to be outgoing, and perhaps I'm a bit cowardly, afraid to face my feelings alone. But there are many people who tend to isolate when they are troubled or who are afraid to trust others with their vulnerability. In the same way that I have invited you to get to know, trust, and love God, I hope that you will be willing to try to overcome your fear and hesitation so you can find a loving friend, family member, support group, or, of course, God to be with you when you're hurting.

There's a saying in Alcoholics Anonymous: "I drink, but *we* stay sober." Members of AA call it a "we program." Nothing has to be faced alone. This sums up the importance of turning to others when life seems too difficult to bear.

By the time my daughter Shaina was born, eight years into my life with God, He had provided me with a circle of loving and spiritual women friends who had become like family to me. Many of them were older women who were like sisters and aunts in my life. Throughout my pregnancy, they had shared their own experiences of pregnancy and childbirth. A week before Shaina decided to enter this world—three weeks early, I might add—I hadn't a clue about the difference between a receiving blanket and an electric blanket. I'd never changed a diaper, and I'm not sure if I'd ever even held a baby. My wise friends gave me a baby shower, presenting me with their love, support, and a wide array of all these foreign items that they knew I would need.

They walked with me as I learned to give my baby a bath; they showed me what to do to quiet her down when she was upset or colicky. They laughed with me when my daughter did or said funny things, and they put up with my endless bragging and showing off and her every accomplishment.

Thirty years ago, when I was in the navy and stationed in Long Beach, California, I began to receive phone calls from Stanley and

Kay, my mother's first cousin and his wife. I'd never met them, and I knew very little about them. This guy would get on the phone with a raspy New York accent and invite me to visit. They lived very close to the Naval Hospital where I worked. I kept thinking to myself, *What on earth would I say to these people? We couldn't possibly have anything in common. I'm a Jewish convert to Catholicism, and I'm in the navy. They'd never understand.*

I kept avoiding Stanley's phone calls, but one day he caught me off guard, and I accepted his invitation. When I got there, I was greeted by Carole, Stanley and Kay's daughter, who was about my age. The first thing I noticed was that she was wearing a Star of David, the symbol of Judaism, which was overlaid with a cross. *Weird!* The next thing I spotted was a statue of St. Francis of Assisi. *Extremely weird!*

Then Kay introduced herself. She was very tall and large-framed, a direct and no-nonsense sort of woman who opened her home to me and welcomed me into her family. Stanley was very short, with white hair, sparkling eyes, and a mischievous sense of humor. By the time we had finished our first meal together, I'd found out that Kay had been a WAC (Women's Army Corps) during World War II and had subsequently worked for many years as a general merchandise manager of the Navy Exchange stores on navy bases throughout the Pacific Rim. As if this weren't enough of a surprise, I discovered that Kay was a lifelong Catholic, and that Stanley had converted to Catholicism when he married her, suffering the rejection and loss of his family of origin as a result.

I felt like Ruth from Old Testament scripture: "Your people are my people . . ." God knew I needed family, and now he had provided me with two families, one of blood and one of friendship.

After I gave birth, Kay and Stanley invited me to bring my baby home to their house. Shaina was so tiny that we set up a bassinet in their dresser drawer. It was a joyful week, surrounded by the love and support of this previously unknown family who had become so close that they were, by then, known to me as Uncle Stanley and Aunt Kay.

Months later, when Shaina was baptized, one of my family of friends designed and sewed a beautiful dress for her. It was cream colored with tiny puffed sleeves, decorated with delicate lace flowers, streamers of ribbon, and lace angels cut from antique doilies left to me by my great aunt. The dress was matched with an impossibly small cap, also covered with lace flowers and more ribbon streamers.

Aunt Kay planned and gave a reception in her home where my two California families came together to celebrate. Sadly, Uncle Stanley died shortly before Shaina's baptism, but Aunt Kay chose to open her home anyway, saying that this is what he would have wanted. This was truly a time when pain shared was cut in half and joy shared was doubled.

You Can't Keep It Unless
You Give It Away

If you have stayed with me this far on my journey, you have met God and come to trust Him and view Him as your friend. You confide in Him and trust His advice because you know that He loves you, wants what is best for you, and has the power to help you follow through. You may have had some rough spots in your relationship with God, but you have worked through them or, at least, you know what to do to heal them. You have a life commitment to God that is binding, much like marriage vows. You have found friends and community support to encourage you and share with you as you carry out your lifelong relationship with God, who is now your Most Significant Other.

It is time to deepen your commitment to God by serving others. The Spirit of God can be found in all of us regardless of our station in life or the particulars of our individual histories. By helping others, we show our love for Him.

I know that when I'm being helpful to others, I'm hanging out with God. When I think about the mentors, guides, teachers, and friends who have been put in my life, I recognize that God's love, wisdom, and grace have been present in each of them. My surrogate mom, Ruthie, taught me how to live, taught me that I was loved by her and by God. She taught me how to be appropriate as a naval officer, how to be a good employee, how to be a responsible adult, how to find God in all the right places. My spiritual directors, Sister Eileen, Martha, and Ruben, were guides into the interior realm of the Spirit, helping me learn to discern God's movement in my life. Father A. taught me how to be a Catholic Christian, sharing articles of faith and tenets of religion. My sorority sister, Jani, and my spiritual direction colleague, Emma, were friends who taught me about loyalty, righteousness, and surrender. All of these people and countless others have freely given me love, taught me to have faith in myself and in God, and encouraged me to grow stronger and to make right decisions. Now it is up to me to give to others those life lessons that have been so generously given to me. By passing on the knowledge of life and love that I gained from them, I reinforce this learning for myself.

You can't keep it unless you give it away.

. . .

God created us with our own personalities, skills, and talents and with knowledge that each of us makes a special contribution. First, you must come to believe that you are special, you have something to offer, and you can make a difference.

Many people have a wide variety of early spiritual experiences. When I was a little girl, I had a dream or a vision. An angel came from heaven to tell me that I was here for something special. That memory and knowledge sustained me through difficult times in my life.

My idea of what that something special is has changed significantly through the years. As a young girl, I had the fairy-tale dream of romance and marriage to Prince Charming. While waiting for him to come along, I attended college.

After graduation, I was going to change the world by loving my class of inner city second-grade children. I was terrible at this because I had no clue that discipline was part of love. My class was completely out of control. If any of the children experienced my love, it was a miracle, since my frustration eventually outweighed love and not much learning took place.

When I was finishing my doctorate, I had grandiose dreams

of being a worldwide lecturer, famed for my original theories and engaging presentations.

All these notions of specialness had everything to do with ego and nothing to do with God or service. I wanted love, recognition, approval, fame, fortune, and greatness. If others benefited as a result, that was all well and good, but they were not my primary motivation. It was not that I didn't value service or want to be a kind, loving, generous person. I did. I just know that my deeper motivations were a bit more on the selfish side.

Once I entered a relationship with God as an adult, I began to be more interested in giving, more concerned for the well-being of others, especially those less fortunate. I came to believe that what is truly special or important in God's eyes was radically different from what I had previously thought. What seemed small or insignificant in my old way of thinking might actually be an important gift to a world in need. Mother Teresa said, "We can do no great things, only small things with great love."

If one person learns to desire God and follow Him because of something I say, is that enough? If another person's relationship with God is healed, is that enough? If I experience something painful and come through it with God's help, then help someone else in a similar situation by sharing my experience, is that enough? If one of my daughter's friends finds a listening ear in me and is able to experience love in my home that has eluded her in her own family, is that enough? If I provide one hamburger from McDonald's to the homeless person standing outside, is that enough? If I give my discarded clothes to the local recovery home, is that enough?

None of these things will bring me fame, fortune, or recognition, but in each of these I am a channel for the expression of God's love.

And that is enough.

. . .

By the time I was a teenager, friends and acquaintances alike told me their problems. I was known to be dependable and reliable, but I never thought I was particularly liked. I thought I would have no friends if I didn't try to make myself indispensable in my friends' lives. I was already playing the role of counselor by the time I was sixteen.

In my late twenties, I worked for my father, who owned a shoe store off Fifth Avenue in New York City. He gave me the title of manager, though there already was one. I spent most of my time vaguely trying to look busy, paying bills and balancing the store's checkbook with questionable success. He gave me a salary and access to petty cash. What a relief! I think he knew I was lost and wanted to protect me.

At that time, I was in group therapy with Deborah, who'd been my friend since we were four years old. One day during group, she looked at me and pointedly asked, "Judith, when are you going to get out of the basement of that shoe store and do something with your life?"

With no small amount of annoyance and defensiveness, I asked her what in the world she was talking about. Deborah was studying to become a ballet dancer. She had been focused on this goal all her life, so she was probably mystified by my apparent lack of goals.

Impatiently, she replied, "Isn't there anything you ever thought of or dreamed about that you would really like to do?"

My response went something like this: "Well, I don't know. I always wished I could draw or be an artist, but I have absolutely no talent in that direction. I can barely draw a stick figure. And I would like to own a restaurant, but I have no money to get something like that going."

Then, in a very small voice, I found myself saying something that I had never previously had any conscious thought about. "I'd kind of like to be a psychologist."

Oh, my God. Did I really say that? Probably everyone will start laughing any minute.

I looked up waiting for the laughter and for my therapist Jon to discourage me. Instead, to my amazement, he (and everyone in the group) encouraged me.

"You'd make a good therapist. You listen well. You're caring. You give good feedback. You're always helpful." And so on. This was amazing to me and downright embarrassing.

Two months later, in order to prove that I could do the work (I had never bothered to try to do well in college), I enrolled in classes toward a master's degree program at Columbia University. And the rest is history!

God had undoubtedly spoken through both Deborah and me. Like a tugboat gently nudging the larger but infinitely less flexible liner into its slip, God was lovingly pushing me onto my right path. And that was back in the days when I was acting as if God was dead! He is definitely able to enter through closed doors.

Though I frequently allow myself to be a channel for God to speak to my patients, I have to guard against the temptation to think that my God-given profession substitutes for service. Many of us in helping professions fall into that error. Though counseling is a ministry, I believe that service I am paid for doesn't qualify as an act of service.

A charitable activity shouldn't be something that you do on a regular basis as part of your occupation. It is important to step outside your comfort zone and be willing to be a bit inconvenienced while endeavoring to make a contribution to the community.

Here are some examples of how you might go out of your way:

- In order to tithe, you might cut something out of your budget or forgo buying a new outfit or theater tickets that you really want but don't need.
- Show up for meetings at your place of worship when you'd rather be home in bed watching your favorite TV show.
- Agree to set up for the fund-raiser potluck on a hot Saturday morning when you'd prefer to be in the swimming pool.
- Go to an earlier worship service so you can provide a ride for an elderly person who can't drive anymore.
- Travel fifty miles in the pouring rain to speak to a group of people about some area of service to which you're devoted.
- Put up with the often depressing atmosphere at a nursing home to read to someone who can no longer see to read.

If you're anything like me, you have lots of excuses to avoid being of service: *I'm too busy. I'm too tired. I have no talent. I have nothing of interest to say. I have no transportation. I don't know how to get involved.*

When I find myself complaining about the inconvenience and I try to justify finding a way out, I pray for a better attitude. When I'm done, I invariably feel warm inside.

I know that when I extend myself to help my sisters and brothers in God's family, something special happens. In each case, the heart speaks and the heart listens, and the world is a bit better for it.

How to Be Charitable

It took me the better part of forever to grow up and become self-supporting. My parents were generous people, and it gave my father great pleasure to give my mother, sister, brother, and me whatever we wanted. I never had to work or contribute in any way to the community of my family. Other than occasional duty drying the dishes or setting the table, I didn't even have chores to do. If it weren't for my nine summers at overnight camp, I probably never would have learned how to make a bed or mop a floor.

I went away to college on a full scholarship, provided not by an institution for my academic achievement, but by the Bank of Dad. This is the way it was done in the community where I grew up, so this is what I expected and thought I was entitled to. I don't think it even occurred to me to be grateful.

In graduate school, I was awarded a teaching fellowship (the equivalent of being a teacher's aide in high school), providing a little money and requiring very little work. I subsidized my fellowship income with a low-cost federal student loan, hoping that I would one day be able to pay it back. My father had experienced some financial setbacks by that time, and my sister and brother-in-law began providing me with a monthly allowance.

If it hadn't been for this help, I don't know if I would have had the wherewithal to go to school *and* work. The abundant generosity I received from my family had done absolutely nothing for my self-esteem.

My emotional stability wasn't the greatest through those years, and I had no real idea of how dependent I actually was. I was never taught the necessary skills for basic adult life.

By the time I graduated from college, I didn't know how to cook, clean, shop, or balance a checkbook. I tried various jobs, but I had no concept of how to take direction. This state of affairs led to my "working" for my dad in his shoe store with limited responsibility in exchange for the money I "earned."

It wasn't until I joined the navy as a psychologist that I learned to be self-supporting through my own contributions, thus finally being able to feel good about myself. I might never have been able to pull this off, either, if it had not been for the generosity, wisdom, and encouragement of Ruthie, my spiritual mentor. Having been the wife of a Marine Corps officer for three decades, she was able to teach me how to survive and even thrive within the military establishment.

At first, I was so unsure of myself that I would work for forty-five minutes, then cry for the next forty-five minutes while I spoke to Ruthie on the phone to get some encouragement and direction about what to do next. I was in a financial mess, having incurred more debt than I could manage and having no idea how to fix it. Once again, Ruthie taught me to trust God, suggested that I get guidance from Consumer Credit Counselors of Los Angeles, and showed me how to budget and save money. Friends gave me their used clothing, and my new family, Aunt Kay and Uncle Stanley, often invited me for dinner.

As I learned and matured, I began to gain self-esteem and the desire to help others to help themselves. Overseeing this whole transformation, of course, was my generous, loving, and wise God.

God wants us to be charitable. Being kind, caring, giving, forgiving, and thoughtful are attitudes central to acts of charity as well as true expressions of unconditional love.

All spiritual traditions value acts of service. In the Jewish community, "doing a mitzvah" has come to mean performing any act of human kindness. The word "mitzvah" actually means commandment, as in God's laws for living, and Jews are commissioned to anonymously care for, clothe, and feed the poor and needy. The highest form of *tzedakah,* or charity, is the provision of a way for people in need to find work or a means to become self-supporting, thus helping those on the margins of society to gain dignity. In Judaism, these kindnesses are a way of obtaining forgiveness for sin.

The more I got to know and trust God, the more I understood that he's the source of all things, but sometimes the channels change. I'll be forever grateful for the many mitzvot and tzedakah that were offered to me, sometimes anonymously, often not, but always with my well-being and growth in mind. The givers were always channels for God's grace.

There are many ways to become charitable. Use the four Ts as your reminder: Tithe your time, talent, and treasure. Here are some suggestions for getting started:

Tithe Your Treasure

- The most obvious method of tithing your treasure is making financial contributions. A New Testament parable tells the story of a widow who gave two small copper coins to the temple treasury. Jesus commented that she gave more than all the others since they gave out of their excess, but she gave all she had. If you have no coins, give someone a flower from your garden, a slice of your bread, a dress you no longer wear. Everyone has something she can let go of.
- If you belong to a church or other religious community where you are being fed spiritually, tithe there. If you don't have a formal organization to give to, then donate to your favorite charities. Or do both.
- If you are afraid to give money because you are struggling to feed your family and pay your bills, experiment with tithing. Start with a small amount, say 1 percent. Then increase the amount as you gain confidence. You might find that when you give a piece of bread, you'll get back a chicken sandwich!

Tithe Your Talent

Everyone has some gift, some ability that can be helpful or inspirational to others. You can share your skills by volunteering at church, the local hospital, or other institutions or organizations. Or you can offer your talent on a one-on-one basis.

- Do you like to write? Offer to contribute an article to your church newsletter. Or help someone reentering the workforce to put together a résumé.
- Do you like to sing? Join the choir or entertain children on a cancer ward or seniors in an assisted living center.
- Do you like to entertain, opening your home to others? Invite people to join in a small faith community at your home: a scripture or spiritual book study, prayer group, or dinner fellowship. Or offer snacks, a table, and chairs for your writing group or book club.
- Are you in recovery from alcoholism or another addiction in a Twelve Step program? Share your experience, strength, and hope at a hospital, recovery home, prison, shelter, or mission. Or, greet a newcomer at a meeting; agree to be a sponsor when asked.
- Do you have construction or fix-it skills? Offer to fix the plumbing at the your place of worship, paint the walls at the homeless shelter, fix the roof at the recovery home. Or assist people who are ill or in pain by making needed home repairs that they can't accomplish or pay for on their own.
- Do you enjoy crafts, knitting, painting, baking, sewing? Make things to sell or give away at a charitable event. Or make presents for needy children and prepare meals to help families to celebrate the major holidays of your faith.

You can tithe your talent and enjoy yourself while receiving joy, gratitude, and fulfillment in the process. What a deal!

Tithe Your Time

This should be one of the easiest things to offer, but in our busy world, it seems almost impossible to find time to spare. Overwhelmed with work, we stay overtime because there are bills to pay or unfinished tasks to get done. More time and energy is often expended traveling long distances in traffic just to get to work. Family needs sap our energy as we cook and clean (sometimes in addition to the day job) and take the kids to soccer, dance, and other activities. It seems impossible to find any leisure time for family to be together. Relationships with spouses and partners suffer because there's no time to talk and there's never time to go out together for dinner or a date. We're told we must take care of our health, so we struggle to make time and take the opportunity to exercise. Oh yes, we are also supposed to save time to pray, meditate, and read scripture. So how can we possibly find time to do service?

- If you are a professional with skills for which you are paid a fee, just fit a needy person into your regular schedule and provide your service for free. You can save a certain amount of time each month for pro bono (no charge) work.
- If you can't give time to work on an event planning committee, offer to help out on the day of the event.
- Offer to come early before your religious service or Twelve Step meeting to shake hands, greet people, or set up. You're going to go there anyway, so just add a half hour or an hour to this already scheduled activity.

I ask God to show me how to make time to give to Him. I know that my God is generous. He doesn't need my time, my talent, or my treasure. So when I offer these things to God, He always gives them back to me with interest. I am the beloved child of a loving God whose good pleasure it is to share His riches with me.

Epilogue

Living with God in the Present Moment

It has been a long journey since I stopped looking for God in all the wrong places, a sometimes exciting, sometimes frightening, always interesting journey. I have shared with you many of my experiences along the way, and I hope you have found useful tools for finding God, coming to know, trust, and love Him. I pray that you have also gained greater self-acceptance as God's beloved child—brave but innocent, flawed but perfect, silly but wise, doubting but steadfastly faithful. I have faith that, as your commitment to God deepens, you will know to the core of your being that He is always with you, always faithful to you, always rooting for you, and always loving you, whether you are experiencing joyful consolation, profound darkness, dull mediocrity, or any state in between.

Today, I find God everywhere, within me, within others, in every circumstance, and in every happening. He's there when friends in my writing group encourage me to keep going when I feel sure I am producing boring drivel. He's there within me when I ask the Holy Spirit to speak God's words through my heart onto the page. He's there when I speak to my patients and when He helps me find something lovable even in the seemingly unlovable. He's there when I'm afraid of confronting the gardener for the mess I found in my previously beautiful yard. He's there when I fear for my daughter's safety. He's there when I'm deeply disappointed, depressed, or angry, helping me keep on even when nothing makes sense.

God's ways are not always my ways, and God's time is not always my time. I want to correct God, send Him a new watch (maybe He needs a Rolex), bargain with Him, yell at Him, turn my back on Him. Yet, He accepts me and loves me just as I am, no questions asked, no conditions.

When my patients come to me with great anxiety, they're usually living in an imagined future, suffering the consequences of events that may never occur. They're living in the never-never-land of the destructive "What if?"

Moses asked God to tell him His name. God replied, "My name is I Am That I Am."

I point out to my patients, and I remind myself, that God's name isn't "I Was That I Was" or "I Will Be That I Will Be." It is "I Am." He is the Eternal Present, and as long as we remain in the present moment, we are safe because we are resting in God.

Saint Thérèse of Lisieux was a twenty-four-year-old Carmelite nun when she died. Before her death, she completed her spiritual autobiography, a task that was often assigned to novice sisters before they took their lifelong vows. In *Story of a Soul,* Thérèse describes living "the Little Way." Every task she undertook, no matter how menial, she did for God. She worked in the laundry for God, took care of the altar for Him, and she undoubtedly swept floors, made beds and cleaned kitchens for Him, always expressing her love for God. She accepted her illness, and as she grew weaker, she suffered lovingly with God in the present moment.

Brother Lawrence, a simple monk from the seventeenth century, trained himself to be in continual conversation with God. This method of prayer is described in the book *The Practice of the Presence of God.* Inviting God into your life, you can talk to him as you eat lunch, drive to work, talk to your boss, play with your children, embrace your spouse.

When I'm in fear, anguish, sadness, longing, or maddening powerlessness or I'm trying to control outcomes with obsessive thought, I practice God's presence, using the Spiritual Drano method I described in chapter 1 of this book. Or I bring myself back to the present moment by saying to myself, *Right here, right now, this one thing I do—I wash this dish. I write this report. I scratch my nose.* And so on.

I've heard it said, "Every moment is a gift from God. That's why it's called the Present." This is my wish for you, that you will live every moment of your life in the Eternal Present, resting in the arms of the great **I AM.**

Appendix 1

My Favorite Prayers

I had some familiarity with the Unity philosophy and spirituality through a daily prayer and affirmation publication called *Daily Word* that I received as a gift from a friend more than twenty-five years ago. Based on the teachings of Jesus, Unity helps people from all faith communities grow spiritually through the use of prayer and affirmation toward a life filled with hope, healing, prosperity, and peace.

I received the Prayer for Protection in response to a call I made to the Unity Prayer Room. I don't remember what I was feeling desperate about, but I do remember the comfort I received when one of the devoted prayer room volunteers spent time with me on the phone praying and reminding me of God's love, care, and protection.

This prayer is very powerful, and I use it frequently. I also share it with my patients when they are overcome with fear or despair.

Sometimes I imagine a line from the prayer, seeing in my mind's eye the light of God surrounding me and feeling the warmth of God's love enfolding me. Sometimes I use it as Spiritual Drano (see chapter 1), repeating all or part of the prayer over and over until I feel balanced and centered.

When I am concerned about someone else, my daughter or a friend, for instance, I say the words of the prayer. Instead of the

pronoun "me," I substitute the pronoun "you" and the name of
the person I am praying for.

Prayer for Protection

The light of God surrounds me.
The love of God enfolds me.
The power of God protects me.
The presence of God watches over me.
Wherever I am, God is.

or

The light of God surrounds you, Ellen (or Mike or
Joanne or Jane . . .).

The Prayer for Protection was written by James Dillet Freeman. It
is used by permission of Unity, www.unityonline.org.

• • •

The Serenity Prayer is widely known and well-loved. It is a gift-
shop staple, almost as ubiquitous as Starbucks coffee. It deco-
rates coffee tables, kitchen walls next to the spice rack, office
desks, and computer screens. The appeal of the first four lines is
universal, not limited to any particular religion, denomination,
or spiritual path.

When Bill Wilson, the co-founder of AA, first heard the Serenity
Prayer, he commented that the first stanza completely summarizes
the philosophy of Alcoholics Anonymous. It has become a part of
Twelve Step meetings around the world, and it is used by many
people in recovery to help them through difficult life situations and
emotional moments.

For me, it is the best reminder that my peace of mind and
sense of well-being depends not on what others are doing or not
doing, saying or not saying, but on my own thoughts, attitudes,
and actions. In other words, the things I can't change are people,
places, and things outside myself. What I can change (with God's
help, of course) is me.

The authorship of the full text of the Serenity Prayer has been a source of debate for the past several decades. It is most commonly attributed to the theologian Reinhold Niebuhr, but even he commented that it might have been around for years, although he honestly believed that he wrote it himself. Many believe that the writer remains unknown.

The entire prayer is presented here, but it is the first four lines that have become a popular part of the culture, particularly in Alcoholics Anonymous.

The Serenity Prayer

God, grant me the serenity
to accept the things I cannot change,
the courage to change the things I can,
and the wisdom to know the difference.

Living one day at a time;
accepting hardships as the pathway to peace;
taking, as He did, this sinful world
as it is, not as I would have it;
Trusting that He will make all things right
if I surrender to His will;
That I may be reasonably happy in this life
and supremely happy with Him forever in the next.
Amen.

. . .

The next two prayers are by Saint Ignatius of Loyola, a soldier turned mystic who founded the Society of Jesus, more popularly known as the Jesuits. I said these two prayers frequently during my first years of pursuing a love affair with God.

When I later experienced disappointment with God, I stopped saying these prayers because they seemed to set a standard that was more saintly than human. I was afraid of what God would give me if I offered all of myself to Him. It might be more than I was willing or able to give.

Through the years I have come to trust that God has a good plan for me, better than anything that I dream up for myself. Now that I am living a comfortable life with God, I am not afraid anymore, and these prayers are regulars in my life.

Take Lord and Receive

Take Lord, and receive
all my liberty, my memory,
understanding and entire will—
all that I have and call my own.

You have given it all to me.
To you, Lord, I return it.

Everything is yours;
do with it as you will.
Give me only your love and your grace.
That's enough for me.

Prayer for Generosity

Lord Jesus, teach me to be generous;
teach me to serve you as you deserve,
to give and not to count the cost,
to fight and not to heed the wounds,
to toil and not to seek for rest,
to labor and not to seek reward,
except that of knowing that I do your will.

Amen.

. . .

This next prayer, like so many of the others that I have grown to love, has a great deal to do with putting ego and selfishness aside in order to nurture attitudes of love and service. Saint Francis of Assisi was from a wealthy family, but he gave up his worldly goods to become an itinerant preacher, teaching God's love of man and all creation.

Having been set to music, it has become a hymn that is often sung in church. Like the Serenity Prayer, the Prayer of Saint Francis is often given as a gift because of the depth of love in its message. Alcoholics Anonymous literature uses this prayer to illustrate how to listen to God through meditation: see *Twelve Steps and Twelve Traditions* (New York: AA World Services, 2002).

The Prayer of Saint Francis

Lord, make me a channel of your peace,
that where there is hatred, I may bring love,
that where there is wrong, I may bring the spirit of
forgiveness,
that where there is discord, I may bring harmony,
that where there is error, I may bring truth,
that where there is despair, I may bring hope,
that where there are shadows, I may bring light,
that where there is sadness, I may bring joy.
Lord, grant that I may seek rather to comfort than to be
comforted,
To understand, than to be understood,
To love, than to be loved.
For it is by self-forgetting that one finds.
It is by forgiving that one is forgiven.
It is by dying that one awakens to eternal life. Amen.

• • •

The Third and Seventh Step prayers of Alcoholics Anonymous are key to the Twelve Step philosophy of recovery. The Twelve Steps are designed to help those seeking recovery from addictions (though they are now widely used to help heal a variety of compulsive or dysfunctional behaviors) find God or a Higher Power and replace self-will with God's will. In the process, people in recovery discover their character defects, which are based on fear and the need to protect the false self, or ego. As a result of the discovery of these shortcomings, the alcoholic (or other troubled individual) becomes able and willing to let go of the traits that prevent full recovery to find true peace with God, and to be of service to others.

Below is a combined version of the Third and Seventh Step prayers of AA that my mentor, Ruthie, taught me. Beautiful prayers, they summarize for those who are seeking to deepen their relationship with God the need to surrender, be of service to others, and gain true humility.

The Third and Seventh Step Prayers (Combined)

Lord, I offer myself to you,
To build with me and to do with me as you will.
Relieve me of the bondage of self that I may better do your will.
Take away my difficulties, shortcomings, defects of character,
all those things that grate upon the sensibilities of others
and that stand between you and me,
so that victory over them may bear witness
to those you would have me help and serve
of your presence, your power, your love, and your way of life.
May I do your will always.
Amen.

• • •

I like to review my day before going to sleep. I look for the moments when God was most present during the day and when He seemed most absent. Generally, when God appears to be absent, it is either because I am not paying attention or because I am running on self-will. When I realize that I have slipped into ego (remember, ego = edging God out!) or fallen short in my attitudes and actions, I run the risk of becoming even more self-absorbed because I am so disappointed in myself.

I want to be able to go to sleep remembering that God loves me exactly as I am. I acknowledge my shortcomings, resolve to do better, and say this comforting prayer taken from John Kirvan's *Let Nothing Disturb You: A Journey to the Center of the Soul with Teresa of Avila* (Notre Dame, IN: Ave Maria Press, 1996, 2007, page 195).

My Day Is Ending (Day Twenty-Eight)

Let nothing, O Lord,
disturb the silence of this night.
Let me not be afraid
to linger here in your presence
with all my humanity exposed.
For you are God—
you are not surprised
by my frailties,
by my continuous failures.
You are my God,
but you are also my friend.
You are on my side;
you will never fail me.
Here in the gathering darkness
I feel able to withstand the whole world,
should it turn against me.
For if I have you, God,
I want for nothing.
You alone suffice.

Appendix 2

Common Defects of Character

When I first tried to identify my defects of character, I was mystified. I had never developed a meaningful vocabulary for talking about personal shortcomings. To be sure, I knew how to put myself down for being stupid, ignorant, fat, klutzy, and so on. But this sort of name-calling was harmful, not helpful. As I read various books, pamphlets, and articles, and as I sought help and suggestions from other people, I got some general ideas to help me talk about shortcomings. The literature of Alcoholics Anonymous gives some clues. It speaks of "one hundred forms of self," "instincts gone awry," "index of maladjustment," "seven deadly sins," and the foursome of selfishness, self-centeredness, fear, and dishonesty.

The problem with these generalities is just that—they are too general. They don't provide me with the sort of personalized, specific information to set me free of the traits that block my ability to see and fully express my good traits. These generalities also don't take into account that God answers prayer. So if I ask God to remove my character defects, He will take me at my word and give me opportunities to give them up. But what if I don't really know what I'm trying to give up except in a general way?

For example, God gave me the chance to let go of the selfish habit of being controlling. But that wasn't on my vague list of character defects, so I had no idea what was going on when my best friend got fed up with me because I was once again insisting that everything go my way. If I had had the vocabulary then to discover the specific defects that apply to me, it would have been easier to see when I was falling into that old attitude, and I could have asked God to save me from my destructive trait of being controlling.

To help myself become clear about the habits, attitudes, traits, shortcomings, deadly sins, or one hundred forms of self, I developed a list of them. In the same way I shop for clothing when I'm not sure what size, color, or design is right, I try out words on the list to see what fits. Before I was able to change, I first had to become aware of what needed changing.

Looking at yourself with this degree of honesty requires courage, willingness, and a loving environment. It is a difficult and painful part of the process of becoming free, developing humility, and ultimately coming to truly know and accept yourself. This is why the support of a kind, gentle, and wise spiritual guide and belief in the love and care of God are essential. Remember, love brings up everything opposite to itself so that love can heal it. This means your character defects.

Here is my list of common character defects (page 157). I developed it to help myself but have also used it to help others. The list is not meant to be discouraging or to bring up old shame. Instead, think of it as a tool to help you achieve true knowledge of what thoughts, attitudes, and behaviors you may need to change so you can see yourself as God sees you.

Common Defects of Character

Arrogance	Intolerance	Shame
Bossiness	Irresponsibility	Slander
Childishness	Judgmental	Sloth
Competitiveness	tendencies	Smothering
Controlling	Lack of acceptance	tendencies
tendencies	Laziness	Spitefulness
Cruelty	Lust	Stinginess
Demanding	Perfectionism	Stubbornness
tendencies	Possessiveness	Superiority
Dependency	Pride	Suspiciousness
Dishonesty	Procrastination	Unfriendliness
Envy	Rebelliousness	Ungratefulness
Gluttony	Rigidity	Unhelpfulness
Gossip	Self-centeredness	Vanity
Grandiosity	Self-hatred	Vengefulness
Greed	Selfishness	Willfulness
Impatience	Self-pity	
Impulsiveness	Self-righteousness	

Excessive fear of:

Abandonment
Being unacceptable
Being unlovable
Financial insecurity
Rejection

Excessive need for:

Approval
Attention
Power
Prestige
Protection

Appendix 3

Suggested Readings

Aaron, Rabbi David. *Living a Joyous Life: The True Spirit of Jewish Practice.* Boston, MA: Trumpeter, 2007.

Alcoholics Anonymous: The Basic Text of AA. New York: Alcoholics Anonymous World Services, 2001.

Allen, James. *As a Man Thinketh.* New York: Barnes & Noble Books, 1992.

De Mello, Anthony. *Sadhana: A Way to God—Christian Exercises in Eastern Form.* New York: Doubleday/Image, 1978.

———. *The Way to Love.* New York: Doubleday/Image, 1995.

Drummond, Henry. *The Greatest Thing in the World.* New York: Grosset & Dunlap, 1979.

Dyckman, Katherine Marie, and L. Patrick Carroll. *Inviting the Mystic, Supporting the Prophet: An Introduction to Spiritual Direction.* Mahwah, NJ: Paulist Press, 1981.

Eisenberg, Ronald. *The 613 Mitzvot: A Contemporary Guide to the Commandments of Judaism.* Rockville, MD: Schreiber, 2005.

Fox, Emmet. *Find and Use Your Inner Power.* New York: Harper & Row, 1979.

———. *Make Your Life Worthwhile.* New York: Harper & Row, 1979.

———. *Power Through Constructive Thinking.* New York: Harper & Row, 1979.

———. *Sermon on the Mount.* New York: Harper & Row, 1979.

Galli, Mark, and James S. Bell, Jr. *The Complete Idiot's Guide to Prayer.* Indianapolis, IN: Alpha Books, 2004.

Green, Thomas H. *When the Well Runs Dry: Prayer beyond the Beginnings.* Notre Dame, IN: Ave Maria Press, 1979.

Hahn, Thich Nhat. *The Energy of Prayer: How to Deepen Your Spiritual Practice.* Berkeley, CA: Parallax Press, 2006.

———. *Living Buddha, Living Christ.* New York: Riverhead Press, 1995.

Hurnard, Hannah. *Hinds' Feet on High Places.* Wheaton, IL: Tyndale House/Living Books, 1975.

Ignatius of Loyola. *The Spiritual Exercises of Saint Ignatius.* Translated by Anthony Mottola. Garden City, NJ: Doubleday/Image, 1964.

John of the Cross. *Dark Night of the Soul.* Translated by Mirabai Starr. New York: Riverhead Books, 2003.

Kabat-Zinn, Jon. *Wherever You Go, There You Are: Mindfulness Meditation in Everyday Life.* New York: Hyperion, 1994.

Keating, Thomas. *Open Mind, Open Heart: The Contemplative Dimension of the Gospel.* New York: Continuum International, 2006.

Kirvan, John. *Let Nothing Disturb You: A Journey to the Center of the Soul with Teresa of Avila.* Notre Dame, IN: Ave Maria Press, 1996.

Kula, Rabbi Irwin, with Linda Lowenthal. *Yearnings: Ancient Wisdom for Daily Life.* New York: Hyperion, 2006.

Kurtz, Ernest, and Katherine Ketcham. *The Spirituality of Imperfection: Storytelling and the Search for Meaning.* New York: Bantam, 2002.

Kushner, Harold. *Who Needs God?* New York: Simon & Schuster, Fireside, 1989.

Lawrence, Brother. *The Practice of the Presence of God.* Translated by Robert J. Edmonson. Brewster, MA: Paraclete Press, 1985.

Lewis, C. S. *The Screwtape Letters.* New York: HarperCollins, 2001.

Merton, Thomas. *Contemplative Prayer.* Garden City, NY: Doubleday/Image, 1971.

———. *Spiritual Direction and Meditation.* Collegeville, MN: Liturgical Press, 1960.

———. *Thoughts in Solitude.* New York: Farrar, Straus and Giroux, 1973.

Nouwen, Henri J. M. *The Wounded Healer: Ministry in Contemporary Society.* Garden City, NY: Doubleday/Image, 1972.

Peale, Norman Vincent. *Positive Imaging: The Powerful Way to Change Your Life.* New York: Ballantine Books, 1982.

Rumi, Maulana Jalal al-Din. *The Essential Rumi.* Translated by Coleman Barks. New York: HarperOne, 1995.

Rumi, Maulana Jalal al-Din, and William C. Chittick. *Sufi Path of Love: Spiritual Teachings of Rumi.* Stony Brook, NY: SUNY Press, 1984.

Swan, Laura. *The Forgotten Desert Mothers: The Lives and Stories of Early Christian Women.* Mahwah, NJ: Paulist Press, 2001.

Teresa, Mother. *Come Be My Light: The Private Writings of the "Saint of Calcutta."* Edited by Brian Kolodiejchuk. New York: Doubleday, 2007.

Teresa of Avila. *The Interior Castle.* Translated by Mirabai Starr. New York: Riverhead Books, 2003.

Thérèse of Lisieux. *The Story of a Soul.* Translated by Robert J. Edmonson. Brewster, MA: Paraclete Press, 2006.

Twelve Steps and Twelve Traditions. New York: Alcoholics Anonymous World Services, 2002.

Wiesel, Elie. *Night.* Translated by Marion Wiesel. New York: Hill and Wang, 2006.

Yancey, Phillip. *Disappointment with God.* Grand Rapids, MI: Zondervan, 1997.

About the Author

As a clinical psychologist and spiritual director, **Judith E. Turian, Ph.D.,** assists her clients in healing by helping them establish or deepen their spiritual lives. When on active duty in the U.S. Navy, Dr. Turian was the clinical director of the Alcohol Rehabilitation Service at the Naval Hospital in Long Beach, California, where she was influenced by the power of Twelve Step spirituality.

Encouraging her patients to practice the spiritual or religious path to which they are drawn, or in which they are already established, Dr. Turian has been instrumental in healing broken relationships with God or religious communities and helping individuals reestablish trust in the Divine.